Salvation LIFE BOOKS

Spiritual Formation

Wesleyan Perspective

SalvationLife.com

G race & peace,

Da

A Method of Thought, Life, and Love
for All Christians

Grace That Grows

Daniel Ethan Harris

SalvationLife Books
P.O. Box 7151
Midland, TX 79708
www.salvationlife.com/books
E-mail: info@salvationlife.com

Contact SalvationLife Books for bulk pricing.

ISBN-10: 0-9984668-1-6
ISBN-13: 978-0-9984668-1-1

Cover design by Roy Migabon (roymigabon.weebly.com)
Cover image by the author.

For Stuart Smith, Kevin Lobello, and Tim Walker
who had faith in me, gave me grace,
and saved my methodism.

Contents

Stir up the spark of grace which is now in you,
and God will give you more grace.

John Wesley

FOREWORD

A MAZING GRACE! We have sung about it for as long as we can remember, yet many of us forget why grace is truly amazing to begin with, and it slips into being another cliché. Moreover, many are guilty of a rather reductionist construal of grace as being something absolutely necessary when we commence our spiritual life with God but seemingly dispensable after that initial experience. In this regard, grace is deemed as some sort of an entrance requirement and hardly as a sustaining dynamic for our entire spiritual journey. Whatever happened to our sung proclamation that the grace which appeared when we first believed is the same grace that safely leads us home?

Such truncated thinking about grace has a cheapening effect: not only does it diminish its power, but worse, it robs us of the prospective reality of the abundant life that God has designed for us to experience. Jesus himself promised: "I have come that [you] may have life, and have it abundantly" (see John 10:10). When we settle for less than this grace-filled, grace-sustained quality of life, we opt for a mediocre, if not altogether defeated Christian existence.

We desperately need a corrective to this distorted and dangerous understanding. Daniel Harris's work in this book serves as a timely reminder of our own need to embrace a more expansive understanding of grace. In writing his book Daniel has done the Body of Christ an important service, if only to educate us all once again on this familiar subject which we claim to know yet evidently fail to appropriate in our daily walk with God. *Grace that Grows* offers us a fresh approach to an old and familiar concept and enables us to delve deeper into its wider meaning.

Daniel's unique treatment of the theme is holistic: an integrated way of thinking, living, and loving that attends to our beliefs, our habits, and our relationships. Drawing primarily from the wealth of insights of John Wesley, the founder of Methodism, and Dallas Willard, a contemporary leader in the spiritual formation movement amongst evangelical protestants, Daniel invites the reader to learn what it means to cooperate with God's generous grace lavished upon us all through Jesus Christ—that is, to allow God's gift of grace to have its life-giving, unhindered work in us. In the final analysis, that is really all we can do, for none of us has what it takes to effect our own transformation. However, we can indeed "create space"—to quote Henri Nouwen's favorite phrase—for God to transform us and enable us to "grow in the grace and knowledge of our Lord Jesus Christ" (see 2 Pet 3:18).

The book challenges us on many fronts. One in particular has to do with the need to rethink our customary notion of salvation as exclusively a one-time event, rather than as a lifelong process—a phenomenon so evident in the pages of Scripture, with particular clarity in the Gospels. The apostle Paul himself admonishes us to keep working out our salvation (by continually cooperating with grace), ever mindful of the fact that it's God, after all, who is at work within us (cf. Phil 2:13). Daniel directs our attention to the more comprehensive meaning of salvation as representing our entire life with God, which starts, continues, and ends in grace. Rightfully and conclusively, he points out that in the Bible "salvation" and "life" are employed synonymously and interchangeably.

For me, what is so attractive about *Grace that Grows* is that the author himself comes across as refreshingly honest in his confessions, very transparent and vulnerable (and if I may add, downright funny at times) in his storytelling and in the way he utilizes his own real life experiences to illustrate his key points. The book is replete with well-chosen metaphors that help elucidate the concepts and bring them down into practical levels. The book is practical through and through. To cite but one shining example, Daniel's excellent chapter on prayer (a topic that was the focus of his previous book) is quite helpful in engaging the reader to try out various spiritual exercises such as the *examen*. Additionally, each chapter ends with an experiential "practice" segment with simple but very doable suggestions for implementation.

I highly recommend *Grace that Grows*. I suspect that no one who takes the message of this book seriously cannot but feel overwhelmed with gratitude for God's abundant supply of grace. For that's exactly how I felt after soaking myself into its rich contents. Thanks be to God! All is grace indeed!

Wil Hernandez, Ph.D., Obl. O.S.B.
Founder and Executive Director of CenterQuest

INTRODUCTION

M Y FATHER POURED THE MAJORITY OF HIS LIFE'S WORK into his fifty-three acre, 2,400-tree pecan orchard. It's a remarkable place. It's in a quiet, rural part of Texas where we don't see much water or otherwise have many trees. In the midst of the noisy lives most of us live, it's a refreshing oasis of quiet. There are plenty of things in nature that God has accomplished on his own, but that orchard isn't one of them, as my dad put about forty years of constant work into it. Those trees would never have just popped up in that place without him. Yet regardless of how much effort he put in, my dad could never *make* those trees grow. All he could ever do was put into place the conditions in which growth could naturally occur. The planting, watering, pruning, and harvesting all required his effort, but all of them together could not produce a single tree. My dad worked hard throughout the process—doing his part—in order to create the space in which the generous work of nature could take place.

There are ways in which you and I are like all of the seeds which grew into all of those trees. We are designed to grow, to be transformed into something that is both the same thing it was before and also something very different. A tree is a very different thing from a seed, yet it's also undeniable that the tree *is* the seed. When you and I grow, we are transformed in to being fully and truly who we already are.

Since we are human beings with the power of choice, there are also ways in which you and I are like farmers. A pecan

can't make the choices involved in leaving itself in the conditions conducive to its own growth, but you and I can.

I've never seen a seed, nor a farmer, who was inherently capable of making a tree. The growth of the seed into the tree by the hand of the farmer is a gift that neither of them carry in themselves and with which both of them need to cooperate. *Grace is God's gift that grows us,* and this book is about how that happens—what the conditions are that lead to us becoming truly and fully who we are in Christ, and how we go about letting God's gift of grace do its life-giving work in us.

There is a way of life available to each of us which naturally leads to our transformation into being the kind of persons who are really what they are meant to be. This includes both being something very different from and also yet very like who we are now. In these pages, we will explore that way of life and how to leave ourselves planted in it for the long haul, letting God's grace take its effect in and through us.

———

Farming and living both require reliable methods. Even if you don't consider yourself to be a particularly methodical person, it's inevitable that you have methods in your life. If you didn't, you would never eat a meal, nor drive a car, nor read a book—nor accomplish much of anything, because life requires reliable methods. Our methods do not need to be complex, and we don't have to think about them all of the time, but we all have plenty of them, and some of them work better than others.

Since the point of this book is that by God's grace and our cooperation with it, we can become fully and truly who we are in Christ, we are compelled to explore a method of how that happens. We will explore this method for how God's grace grows us in three parts:

- *Part One: Accepting Grace* will focus on our thinking/our beliefs.
- *Part Two: Practicing Grace* emphasizes our living/our habits.
- *Part Three: Giving Grace* explores our loving/our relationships.[1]

I'm certainly not the first person to explore a method for our lives with God, and one group that did so effectively in the past was John Wesley and those who were part of his early Methodist movement. Part of the intent of this book is to help Christians of any tradition rediscover the reliability of the method of the early Methodists.

There have also been plenty in more recent times who have explored and experienced this grace-full kind of life with God, and many of them have never been associated with any group using the term "Methodist." A number of people who have been most helpful in introducing me to this method have been part of what has often been called the "spiritual formation movement" through the past few decades. Much of the intent of this book is also to explore the core of that movement, particularly as it was lived and taught by Dallas Willard.

Willard, Wesley, and countless other followers of Jesus before and after them have been less interested in promoting any institution or particular group within Christianity than they have been in experiencing and sharing the deep goodness of life with God offered to us through Christ, and I want this book to share that spirit. Therefore, if you desire that kind of growth—whatever kind of Christian you may be—this book is intended for you.

Part One

ACCEPTING GRACE

One

GRACE

*From his fullness we have all received, **grace** upon **grace**.*
John 1:16

*By the **grace** of God, this one thing I do: ...I see God, I love God, I serve God. I glorify him with my body and with my spirit.[2]*
John Wesley

*You will consume much more **grace** by leading a holy life than you will by sinning, because every holy act you do will have to be upheld by the **grace** of God.[3]*
Dallas Willard

M Y DAD'S PECAN ORCHARD is my favorite place on earth. Even though he put about forty years of constant work into that orchard, he knew that he could not make a single pecan tree grow. All that he could do was plant the trees in the conditions conducive to their growth, knowing that the actual work of growth was not up to him. Neither was it up to the seeds. Their growth was a gift.

There are ways in which you and I are like all of those pecan seeds, and the image I want us to have in our minds for grace is this: if you and I are the seeds, *grace is God's gift that grows us.*

One way in which we are the seeds is that we are designed to grow. If a pecan in its shell (or any other kind of seed) always remains a pecan inside a shell, it will never experience its life to the full. We could say that it will never know true and full pecan-ness. Looking at the thousands of trees in a full orchard is a different experience than looking at buckets full of seeds. Yet it's also easy for us to understand that those trees in my family's orchard today still are the pecan seeds that were planted there more than forty years ago. If the seed is put into the conditions for its growth, and then allowed to stay there long enough for the gift of life to come to it and take its effect, then—over time (and sometimes it seems like long, slow time)—the seed becomes the tree. In fact—we could say that it becomes more fully what it already is. It's clearly transformed, but those trees are also still the pecans that were planted.

When you or I are planted, and then allowed to stay in the conditions for our own growth long enough, God's generous gift of life comes. Grace comes. Over time, you (the seed) are transformed into the true and full you (the tree). That tree is still you, but it's the you that is truly and fully who you are in Christ—the you grown and growing in God's grace.

> *That tree is still you, but it's the you that is truly and fully who you are in Christ—the you grown and growing in God's grace.*

You and I are the seeds in the grace-driven process of becoming the trees.

———

My guess is that this might be a different way of talking about grace than what is familiar to many of us. The ways that we typically talk about grace stop short of the seed becoming fully what it is. In this metaphor, we usually only talk about grace as having to do with getting the seed into the ground. A seed's planting is an indispensable part of the process of its transformational growth, but the growth and transformation are still yet to come. If we reduce grace to being about our planting as seeds, rather than it being God's gift that grows us, we will simply never have the opportunity to know what it means to *live* by God's abundant grace, which alone can lead us into fully and truly becoming who we are in Christ.

One day a friend and I were talking about having grown up going to church, and we were certainly both deeply grateful to have done so. One of the things that both of us picked up along the way was the version of Christianity that goes something like this: you're a really bad sinner, and Jesus died on the cross so that you could be forgiven. Therefore, you need to ask him to forgive your sins so that you'll get into heaven when you die.

Then my friend made the following observation:

Something that seems to make more sense is to think of it like a marriage. Forgiveness in a marriage is kind of like the foundation poured for a house—there's no chance for the marriage to exist without forgiveness in place. A marriage has to have forgiveness to begin, and it has to have forgiveness to keep going, but forgiveness isn't the marriage.

I realize that it may seem like my aim is to use as many metaphors as possible, but they all point to the same reality: the mature pecan tree is impossible without the seed being planted in the soil, but planting a seed in the ground and having a tree to harvest aren't the same thing. The house is impossible without the foundation, and forgiveness isn't the marriage.

My friend probably didn't realize it, but he certainly wasn't the first to compare life with God to a marriage. If that metaphor isn't your favorite, pick a different relationship. Many images are used in Scripture and Christian tradition to help us understand what the life God intends for us is like: God is a loving parent and we are beloved children; we are friends who walk and talk together; or—back to the marriage metaphor—we are like two people whose lives are meant to become so interwoven with each other that there are no longer barriers between where one life ends and the other begins.

Though a marriage must have forgiveness, forgiveness isn't the marriage. Though we desperately need God's pardon, being forgiven doesn't constitute the life with God which we are offered. Rather, our lives are meant to become so interwoven with God's life that there are no longer barriers between where God's life ends and ours begins.

> *Our lives are meant to become so interwoven with God's life that there are no longer barriers between where God's life ends and ours begins.*

For many of us, our framework for Christianity is often, "Have your sins forgiven so that you can get into heaven when you die." Or for others, it is ultimately about doing good and showing kindness to those around us. Either way, we often reduce the meaning of grace to only meaning forgiveness and/or acceptance. We often talk about grace as essentially meaning God's willingness to forgive us even though we really, really, really don't deserve it. Of course we don't deserve God's forgiveness. Plus, I don't have a chance at becoming anything good without forgiveness. I'm absolutely desperate for it, whether we're talking about my life with God, or with my wife, neither one of those central parts of my life stand a chance without that most foundational of gifts, forgiveness and acceptance. But there is much more to the life God wants to give us by grace. Forgiveness is an incredibly gracious thing of God to offer, but grace is much bigger, and much richer, than just being forgiven.

If forgiveness is such an essential part of a marriage, and an essential part of our lives with God, it's like the seed being planted in the soil. We cannot do without it. That seed going into the soil is an irreplaceable part of its becoming fully what it is. Forgiving acceptance is an indispensable part of us becoming fully and truly who we are in Christ. If grace is God's gift that grows us, an indispensable part of that gift will be the unbelievably good news that God loves us just like we are. (Yes, that means you. Yes, that means me. Yes, that means your neighbor. It means everyone.) It's indescribably good news that this forgiving acceptance is a gift freely given to us, and that we can give up all of our attempts to earn it.

If we are going to experience the life to the full that Jesus said he came to give, however, we must realize that grace goes on, beyond the foundation being poured and beyond the marriage vows being said—beyond the seed being planted in the soil. Once the forgiving acceptance is given, the two lives in the marriage are given a chance to become one. Once you and I as seeds are planted in the ground, we are given the chance, by grace, to not just stay a forgiven and planted seed, but to truly and fully become who we are in Christ.

As Dallas Willard simply and profoundly says, "Grace is about help, not just forgiveness."[4]

———

Dallas' definition of grace helps us to get past the reduced versions of it: "Grace is God acting in our lives to bring about what we do not deserve and cannot accomplish on our own."[5] Grace seen in this way is much bigger, deeper, and wider than just forgiving acceptance. If it is by grace that we are saved through faith in Christ, and grace is God's gift that grows us (including forgiveness, but all the way from being the seed to being the tree, all the way from being someone forgiven of sin to being truly and fully who we are in Christ) then living by grace is such a wonderful, generous invitation for us!

What could be better than the invitation we are given to "grow in the grace and knowledge of our Lord and Savior Jesus Christ"?

Once we hear the goodness of this, and understand something of the magnitude of grace in this way, we can make sense of, and be awed by, passages that really don't make much sense if grace is only about the opportunity to be accepted. Instead, it can give us some freshly opened eyes and ears to see and hear what the Scriptures are saying if we look at grace as God's generously-given help that brings life/God's gift that grows us/God's action in our lives. Then the deeply good news of passages like this can penetrate us in a different way:

"From [Jesus'] fullness we have all received, grace upon grace."

How *generous* is that? There is no scarcity with God's grace! There is no limit to the availability of God's help, God's gift that grows us into who we truly are. Rather than being like a rationed medication, we receive grace *from Christ's fullness, lavished on us.*

———

To help us make an important shift, we might also want to reflect on this:

"...where sin increased, grace abounded all the more."

If we are going to be able to understand and live by the limitlessly good gift that God's grace is—if we're going to be able to make any sense of it in order to be able to shape our lives around it—one of the main ways we need to understand God's grace and how it works is in relation to our sin.

This is where different understandings of grace warp well-intentioned Christians into being soldiers endlessly in battle with one another, with the world around us, and with ourselves. Many conservative Christians view grace as a solution for our personal sins. ("I did this, and I don't deserve to be forgiven for it, but God gives grace.") Many progressive Christians view grace as a solution for our societal sins. ("We did this, and therefore we need to be gracious to one another to right the wrong.")

Regardless of where we are on that spectrum, we usually agree (with some good reason based on our experience) that the thing that separates us from God is our sin. Without question, sin and separation are related to one another. However, if Saint Paul's statement is true that "where sin increased, grace increased all the more, so that, just as sin reigned in death, so also grace might reign through righteousness,"[6] part of what that means is that our separation from God—and our sin—are both significantly different than we think, just as grace is also so much bigger than we usually understand. Grace is given so generously, accessible in abundance, able to do more in us than we realize, available to us long before we know anything about it, as God's great, lavish gift to us every day of our lives—and this is true for every single human being.

Because of that, I think James Bryan Smith hits the nail on the head when he says, *"It is not my sin that moves me away from God, it is my refusal of grace, both for myself and for others."*[7]

That's such a massive shift in how I think about myself and about others. It's a shift in what I believe about how God thinks about me and about everyone I will encounter today. It's a shift in how I think about my sin and the sin evidenced in today's news, and how I expect that God wants to deal with all of it.

For much of my life, my approach to trying to live devoted to God was really about doing my best to avoid sin. When that is the case, we can become obsessed with trying to figure out the right place to draw the lines about what is sin and what isn't.

In this way that we normally think about sin, it's as if God has his official "don't do these things, and I really mean it" list, then we make our best guesses at what is supposed to be on our copies of the list. Then, we 1) hope that our list is close enough to God's to get us by and out of too much trouble, and 2) even if our list turned out to be identical to God's, we wonder if we'll actually be able to stay away from the things on it.

Anyone who has tried approaching the Christian life that way, as I have, knows that it does not work very well. Our list is never exhaustive enough to keep us out of everything, and then we keep getting back into the things that we know are on the list anyway. So, I propose we take a completely different approach and get rid of the conception of sin as the list of "don'ts," and instead, start to *think of sin as anything that chokes God's life in us and keeps it from growing,* anything that blocks God's help toward us, anything that puts a plug on the grace that's available to flood our lives and our world.

When we stop refusing grace and begin to arrange our lives around cooperation with it, we will progressively become more aware of different kinds of things in our lives that might be obstructing grace's flow into and through us. Some of these things may be of the obvious types, which would have appeared on everyone's copies of the "don't" list. If, for example, I am involved in temple prostitution, or strategizing for genocide, it won't be hard to identify a good starting place in removing the grace-obstructions in my life.

But what if we change our entire model of living a devoted life? What if instead of defining it as aiming to *avoid* sin, we look at it as a life of aiming to *cooperate* with God's grace?

> *What if instead of aiming to avoid sin, we aim to cooperate with God's grace?*

If we devote ourselves to learning to cooperate with God's gift that grows us, and we realize that *anything* that chokes God's life in us is sin for us, then we will also begin to be aware of some more subtle blockages to grace. These are kinds that might not show up on the lists of obvious ones. They could be anything—even innocent or legitimately very good things can be blockages to grace. Maybe it is something as innocent as a socially acceptable time-sucker like social media, or it might be something like giving too much attention to our favorite sports team, or our work, or to volunteering to help people. Anything, when misused, can be turned into a grace-blocker.

Here is where it can get particularly tricky, and even particularly dangerous: *We can misuse something spiritual so that the very things that are given to us to be the channels of grace into our lives can paradoxically become its deterrent.* Jesus talks about this in the Sermon on the Mount. The passages may sound familiar: "don't give like the hypocrites do, but give like this....don't fast like the hypocrites do, but fast like this....don't pray like the hypocrites do, but pray like this...." and he went on to teach us the Lord's Prayer.[8]

Let me show you what I mean: a few years ago, I had just published my first book, and its subject was on prayer. For a while afterward, I was blogging about an experiment of trying to pray written prayers, four times a day, every day, without ever missing. That experiment didn't make it through the full year that I intended, and as you'll read below, that's not a bad thing. This is what happened, as I wrote about it on the blog:

Any year-long experiment is bound not to go smoothly through its entirety. At least I hope that's true, since this one was sailing along until my wife said these words to me on Christmas night: "I don't want to be married to a monk, I want to be married to you!...Your experiment is getting on my nerves."

And I admit, she said that for good reason. It turns out that having my prayer book open on the table next to me and trying to discretely turn pages while children were digging into their stockings on Christmas morning in order to squeeze my morning prayer in was a bad idea. Really bad. It might go down with some of my worst.

I quickly realized it was a bad idea when she gave me a look after she saw me doing it, not because she gave me a look, but because I knew it was missing the point. Much of the reason I'm doing this experiment is because of my conviction that praying in these ways will help me be more attentive to God and to those around me—especially my family—in every kind of moment in our lives. Yet there I was on Christmas morning flipping pages rather than paying full attention to my family. (I knew it had been a really bad idea that night when she admitted she's fantasized about ways to go about hiding my prayer book from me.)

Family is where the rubber meets the road in this project. I hope to be doing this ultimately for the benefit of others—hoping that these are means of planting me more firmly in God's kingdom, and that it will therefore make my existence in this world more beneficial for others—most of all these others who live under this roof with me. If I come to the end of this year and my wife isn't glad that I've done this experiment (or before then, if I ever have to go out and buy another copy of my prayer book because she's followed through on her fantasy and destroyed my current one), if it doesn't help me become a better, more loving and attentive husband and father, this experiment of testing my own advice to its farthest reasonable limits will clearly not have been successful. (But in the book's defense, nowhere in Live Prayerfully *do I offer advice that comes anywhere close to flipping through a prayer book while your family is opening Christmas presents. That isn't even included in the "farthest reasonable limits" of what I recommend. That's just an example of the centuries-old practice of engaging in something "spiritual" while completely missing the point of why we do so.)"[9]*

So there is your peek into the Harris family in all of its glory. I hope it makes the point that when we look at sin as the big list of don'ts, probably none of us would put "prayer" on the "don't do this" list. Nonetheless, I have prayed in ways that were obstacles to grace rather than opening its floodgates. Or, I've done innumerable things that wouldn't make anyone around me question my character yet were still done out of a choice to try to satisfy myself rather than find my satisfaction in God, and therefore choked God's grace.

I have also done some of the things that would appear on nearly everyone's copies of the "don't" list, and those absolutely block God's grace as well. However, I think those big, obvious failures are almost always surface expressions, symptoms of the more subtle ways we have chosen to live as if this grace that grows us wasn't so abundantly, lavishly, lovingly available to us in Christ.

The realization that anything can be a grace-blocker can make a tremendous difference in our ability to be genuinely compassionate toward others. Rather than convincing myself that I can see so clearly what another person's grace-obstructions are, my own ongoing experience with God will teach me first, that my "surface sin" always has another, more subtle distortion lying behind it which is blocking the work of grace. Then we can also realize that even the lenses through which I am looking at another person are constantly blurred by the effects of my own issues.

When we can make that shift from thinking about sin as the things on the "don't" list that we need to work so hard to avoid, to thinking about our task as cooperating with grace, doing so will naturally include identifying and removing any obstacles to grace in our lives. As God shows these obstacles to us, over time we will be surprised to find that doing the stuff on the "don't" list—even the ones that really have plagued us—simply won't seem as appealing to us as they once did. That is because the longer we cooperate with grace, like a stream that slowly and gradually, yet forcefully, removes the obstructions in its path, God's grace also naturally goes through the process of dealing with the more subtle kinds of obstructions in its way. The totality of the obstructions and their effects on us and our relationships are never completely gone, because seemingly every time grace wears one away, another becomes apparent. Yet all the while, the channels become more open for God's grace to do what the gracious

God always intends: bring abundant life, to grow us into truly and fully being who we are in Christ.

———

Just for good measure in a chapter already overly packed with metaphors, I'll add one more.

My soul without God is like an old house where no one has lived for decades, all boarded up and dark on the inside. Its structure is still sound, but for whatever reason, no one lives there and so all of the windows and doors have been covered and no light has been allowed in. The house is pretty useless without light; it was intended to be lit up.

Sunlight that is all around the house. It has been there every day, available to penetrate the house's darkness, but blocked out because there is no life in the house and barriers have been built up to keep out intruders, animals, rocks from the neighborhood boys, and also consequentially, the light that could bring life.

If my soul is the darkened house, then God's grace is the sunlight constantly available to stream past the barriers and empower life in that house.

God's grace, the light, is lavishly, generously, lovingly available to come into my darkened house, and eventually, God's light so fills that house that the darkness has been driven out from every room, and it is again a house suitable for life. (We will talk later about what we actually do in the process of removing the boards to let the light in.)

———

Practice

Sometime during the day today, find about five minutes of quiet to unhurriedly reflect on this statement: "Your grace is sufficient for me."

You may find it helpful to do so by emphasizing a different word each time you prayerfully think through this verse of Scripture. For example:

Your grace is sufficient for me.

Your *grace* is sufficient for me.

Your grace *is sufficient* for me.

Your grace is sufficient *for me*.

Two

SALVATION

*Turn, O LORD, **save** my life;*
deliver me for the sake of your steadfast love.
Psalm 6:4

Salvation...*is not...going to heaven....It is not a blessing on the other side of*
death....It is not something at a distance: it is a present thing,...the entire work
of God, from the first dawning of grace in the soul till it is consummated in
glory.[10]
John Wesley

*The simple and wholly adequate word for **salvation** in the New Testament is*
"life."[11]
Dallas Willard

MY LIFE AS AN OLD HOUSE—that's where we left the previous chapter's discussion of grace and where we will pick up now with salvation. Repetition is underrated, so here's some of what we said to close the last chapter, but with some more pieces added to the metaphor.

I like to think of it like this: My soul without God is like an old house where no one has lived for decades, all boarded up and dark on the inside. The house is pretty useless without light; it was intended to be lit up. Its structure is still sound, but for whatever reason, no one lives there and so all of the windows and doors have been boarded up and no light has been allowed in.

God's grace is like the sunlight that is all around the house. It has been there every day, available to penetrate the house's darkness, but blocked out because there is no life in the house and barriers have been built up to keep out intruders, animals, rocks from the neighborhood boys, and also consequentially, the light that could bring life.

If my soul is the darkened house and God's grace is the light that empowers life in that house, then as grace is allowed in, the house is delivered from a process of rotting and into a process of restoration. It is delivered from its own inevitable destruction and into life—into being fully what it is. Eventually, God's light so fills that house that the darkness has been driven out from every room, and it is again a house suitable for life.

If the light that enables life in the house is grace, then what does it mean to say that our salvation is by grace? If God's grace is the light that brings the gift of life, then salvation is the process of the old house being restored, being rescued, being delivered from its own decay and being made new again, infused by life to match the purposes of its creator.

Think of how many things the process of an old house's salvation include. Some buyer sees the house falling apart and knows that it can be restored, and so someone buys it and goes to work. The obstacles that keep light from entering the house come down. Broken parts get fixed. Stuff that doesn't work anymore is taken out—some of it gently, and some of it by being ripped out. New, reliable things are brought in as part of the long process of life coming back into the house. Life eventually spills out of the house as well, with grass, flowers, and other signs that life is happening here.

None of that happens if the house had never been built in the first place. Neither does any of it happen without everything that was part of the house's story prior to the buyer finding it in its run-down state. Everything in the house's story is part of its rescue to life, and that renovation is a long process.

When we talk about salvation in church, we often talk about either stuff in the past (which gets described as "when we got saved"), or in the future, referring to who will or will not make the cut and get into heaven when we die. But both of those ways of talking about what it means to be saved by grace are incomplete. Since they're incomplete, they end up missing the point and leading us on unhelpful detours.

Think of it with this house. If we were to ask the house our equivalent of, "When did you get saved?" we are probably asking about the date when the buyer who would restore the house went to the title company and purchased it. When did ownership of the house change? Or, to look at salvation as the equivalent of getting into heaven after we die, perhaps the owner throws a big party after the renovation is complete. Yet neither of those moments are the story of the house's restoration. Both of them are part of how the house was delivered from decay into life, but they leave out the process that encompasses both of those moments.

Or, let's look at it through our seed metaphor. I said in the previous chapter that the ways we often talk about grace reduce it to forgiveness—to the first step in the process. We reduce it to the decaying house being purchased or the seed being planted in the ground. Obviously none of the rest of the story is possible without that happening, without the house being bought by someone who could restore it, or without the seed being planted in the soil. Even so, the moment the pecan trees were planted in their past (as undeniably essential and wonderful as that moment is) is one part of the process of them becoming fully what they are. That full process of their deliverance from being a seed, just trapped in its shell, to being fully alive, is a long process.

That long, grace-driven process, when God's lavish, generous, and loving gift grows us into fully and truly who we are in Christ—that process is our salvation. *If grace is God's gift that grows us, salvation is deliverance into life.* That all happens as a gift. The pecan tree is powerless to come out of the shell of the seed on its own. It needs grace. The house can't stop decaying and restore itself—it needs light to come in by the hand of a capable restorer. You and I cannot deliver ourselves from our own patterns that destroy us, our own self-interest, our own lack of ability to love. We have to be delivered into really being alive, and that only happens as a wonderful, rich gift of grace by God. Although there are particular landmarks along the way, it is always a process.

Theologian Scot McKnight talks about this contrast between looking at salvation as a moment—either in our past or in our future—versus understanding and participating in it as a process. He says,

> *Salvation has three tenses in the New Testament. Biblical salvation is salvation times three.*
>
> *Past: We have been saved (Romans 8:24).*
> *Present: We are being saved (Philippians 2:12).*
> *Future: We will be saved (Romans 13:11).*
>
> *Add these together and you come up with something vitally important for life...salvation is a process, not a one-time, one-and-done event. It takes, one might say, a lifetime and beyond to get saved.*"[12]

McKnight then goes on to point to the central Biblical image of salvation, which is the story of the Exodus. God's people were enslaved, and God delivered them, leading them to a life of freedom. So many of the ways that the New Testament speaks of Jesus' role in our salvation also point back to that story of the rescue of God's people from slavery into life in the promised land. In other words, Jesus' role in our salvation is interpreted and understood in light of the Exodus: Moses led God's people from slavery in Egypt to life in the promised land, and that was the framework they found to understand what Jesus did—rescuing us from slavery to sin and death, and delivering us into life as part of God's new creation.

McKnight proceeds. He says,

Realize that it took the Israelites forty long years to get from Egypt to the Promised Land, and that is perhaps the parable we need—that redemption is a process over the journey of a life. The children of Israel didn't pass through the Red Sea to hear the Ten Commandments and then immediately achieve sanctification. That took time, and we are in that time right now, the time where new creation life begins to bubble up into us and into our church fellowship.[13]

You and I get to participate in God's work of making all things new. Like the seed becoming a tree and the house under renovation, we become evidences of God's project of new creation. We see the effects of grace in new lives—new *everything*—as God continues this bigger-than-we-understand work of grace and makes all things new again. In God's generosity, we are delivered from the bondage of our lives without grace (like the seed in its shell), or from the decay of our souls when we refuse God's help (like the dilapidated house)—and into *life*, into being truly and fully who we are in Christ.

I have been saved. I am being saved. I will be saved. All three tenses of that verb happen as we cooperate with God's life-giving gift of grace, given so generously and lavishly to us.

———

I remember pretty clearly how monumental of a shift it was for me to encounter this understanding of salvation. I grew up with the understanding that salvation was about when I was saved (meaning the moment in the past when I asked for forgiveness of my sin), and that it was about who would make the cut in the future and get into heaven after we die. *I really had no idea what my life today had to do with salvation.* Then I was reading one of Dallas Willard's books, *The Spirit of the Disciplines,* and he had a chapter in which he explained this, titled, "Salvation is a Life." It certainly isn't the only time this happened for me with Dallas, but that chapter—and even just the idea of the chapter's title—opened up so much for me. It made sense of much of the Scriptures, and unlocked much of my own experience of life with God. The first sentence in his chapter is, "Why is it that we look upon our salvation as a moment that began our religious life instead of the daily life we receive from God?"[14]

It was a huge shift for me. I found it deeply helpful to understand that God is saving me today, and though this salvation is entirely God's gracious gift, I have a role to play in this process of salvation by cooperating with grace. Or as Paul describes it, to continue to *work out* our salvation, knowing that it's God that *works in* us.

The previous chapter and this one are pretty heavy on theory, and we will turn a corner toward practicality in the next four chapters to emphasize how we work out what God works in. For now, though, I'm just remembering how liberating and empowering it felt to look at salvation in this way. *Salvation by grace isn't just about being forgiven and accepted—it's about a life with God.* It's about cooperating with grace and allowing God to do wonderful, creative work.

Dallas' chapter stuck with me deeply enough that years later I started writing a blog and wanted to name it after that chapter and call it "Salvation is a Life." I didn't want to plagiarize quite that obviously, however, so I just called it SalvationLife, because if there is anything good that I want to communicate there, it's this: our life with God is not just about being forgiven. It isn't just about getting into heaven when we die. It's about a life into which God graciously invites us, a life in which grace grows us into being truly and fully who we are in Christ.

We have been saved. We are being saved. We will be saved.

————

I remember a point as a teenager, when I had an honest desire to live my life the way God wanted me to live it. I had made the kinds of decisions encouraged at church camps, and I was sincere about them.

In the terms that we have been talking about in this chapter: in my mind then (and according to the models that were being given to me) I had been saved. There was a point in my past when I had asked for God's forgiveness (actually, quite a number of those points, and I never was really sure which one mattered the most to God—but I had a number of them just to be on the safe side). As far as I knew, and according to my teachers and preachers, there would also be a future point of salvation. Since I had done what needed to be done to make sure that the future salvation was taken care of, I could rest assured that I would make the cut and be on the right side of the pearly gates when all of this would be over. So there was the past aspect of salvation (having my sins forgiven) and the future aspect (getting into heaven) and those two things were really the entirety of salvation as I understood it. That left the totality of my day-to-day life untouched by my salvation.

I remember a particular day as a teenager when I had a feeling of, "Now what do I *do*? What's my life supposed to be like now that I've decided to give my life to Jesus?" I had made the decision to spend *eternity* with him, but what I really wanted was an answer for what to do with him *today*. I remember even going into the Christian bookstore and hoping to find a book with a title something like *How to Live as a Christian*.

I didn't find any such book then, and although I have had some great guidance from family and friends through every stage of my Christian life, it took me a long time (years, if not a decade) to find a way to begin to answer that question in a satisfactory way. When I did begin to discover an answer, it had to do with this: salvation is a life. It isn't just about being forgiven, but it's about the entirety of the ways that God works through grace to deliver me into fullness of life. God's grace is always on offer, abundantly, lavishly available as a gift to grow me. When I cooperate with it, I am in that process of being renovated, being made new, being delivered from that shell and grown into truly and fully who I am in Christ.

———

There is a very important implication of this, which may already be stirring on some level in your mind. It's a shift that is difficult for many of us to make since the view of salvation as being forgiven of our sin so that we can get into heaven when we die is so ingrained in many of us. To make this shift, we need to move toward understanding and living salvation in a way that incorporates forgiveness and the rest of eternity, but which has as its focal point the daily life that we draw from God.

> *We need to move toward understanding and living salvation in a way that incorporates forgiveness and the rest of eternity, but which has as its focal point the daily life that we draw from God.*

When we do so, our bottom line changes. Our tendency is to draw the elemental question as, "Okay, all of this discipleship stuff is great for those who are really into it, and I hope that I get around to it one of these days, but what really, ultimately matters is: who gets in at the end of it all and who doesn't?" If salvation is a life, then that is always the wrong question. Or to say it another way, any questions about, "Can such and such type of a person really be a Christian?" or "Could such and such type of a person be in heaven?" are always missing the point.

Instead, let's accept salvation in all three of its tenses:

God has acted in the past to save all of us, in more ways than we will ever be aware, and most especially in the life, death, resurrection, and ascension of Christ.

In the present, you and I can learn to draw our daily life from God in total dependence on God's grace. We are meant to live like branches do from their vine, allowing the good gift of grace to do its work, growing us into who we are in Christ. It is then that we experience the daily reality of grace as God saving, delivering, rescuing and renovating us.

Then, as God has acted to save us in the past, and has saved us through every day of our present reality as we have opened ourselves to his gift of grace, without a doubt—God will take care of us in the future.

In other words, the bottom line question that really matters is not about who makes the cut, but rather, "Am I cooperating today with God's gift of grace?" If so, then the past, present, and future realities of God's salvation are each taking their effect.

The idea that salvation is not a one and done event, but is rather all of God's work of grace to deliver us into full life, is one common assumption we need to overcome if there is to be any real connection between salvation and our daily lives. But it isn't the only one.

If we are going to be able to live this salvation-life, our thinking about God's offer of salvation as only having to do with *me*, *my* sin, and *my* life has to be re-examined. Before I explain, please do not hear me as trying to undermine the immense importance of settling into the reality of God's love for you as an individual, and God's presence and activity in your own, very personal and private life. Rather than diminishing that, we want to experience it to its full, and to experience it, we have to take a good look at how that can actually happen. The point I want to make is this: Yes, God has saved *me*, is saving *me*, and will save *me*, but that never happens with *me* in isolation. Rather, the *me* that God loves and delivers into life is always a me that is part of God's much larger people—a people whom God has saved, is saving, and will save and deliver into life. Indeed, even this much larger whole of God's people is one part of the even larger totality of all of God's creation. God, in immense grace, has saved, is saving, and will save, delivering all of creation—including us (individually and en masse)—into life. God never intended for me to become truly and fully who I am in Christ by myself. That only happens in relationships with others who are also in the same process of growth in grace.

Initially, I thought that this was an area where my metaphor of the pecan seeds and trees would break down, because one solitary pecan can obviously grow into one pecan tree if it remains in the right conditions.

However, then I remembered my dad saying something about male and female trees, which I never really understood, but it surprised me and so I looked it up. It turns out pecan trees can teach us quite a bit about the necessity of community in God's work of saving grace.

If you are walking through a Texas neighborhood, it is very possible that you might see one pecan tree by itself. However, if you see that solitary pecan tree, you can immediately conclude its original seed has not fully become what it had the potential of becoming when it was planted. That tree is not as healthy and not producing the quality of nuts that it could have, because to be fully delivered from their seed-shells and into their pecan-lives, those trees need other trees around them that are in the same process.

As I remembered my dad's comment and did some research, what I discovered was pretty fascinating. Apparently the trees all have male and female parts. The male buds on the trees release the pollen, and the female buds end up producing the pecans. If that happens within one solitary tree, it's about as effective as inbreeding with animals. However, if the trees are in an orchard, they learn to time their budding so that some trees will release their pollen at the same time that other trees are ready to receive it. Then, later, they switch roles—the receiver trees turn into the pollen producers, and the others are ready to receive. Then, all of the trees, *because of their proximity to one another as they grow,* can become more fully what they are in their pecan-ness in ways that would not be possible if they were alone.

Just like those seeds, I am not saved by myself. I do not cooperate with grace by myself. You and I can only become truly and fully who we are in Christ as we have been saved, are being saved, and will be saved *with each other*. We just aren't designed for it to work any other way.

———

Practice

The quote from Dallas Willard at the beginning of this chapter indicates how strong of a connection the New Testament makes between God's offer of salvation and God's gift of life. One of the things that set me up for this big shift from looking at salvation as an event in the past or future to the daily life I draw from God was, following a suggestion from Dallas' books, repeatedly reading big chunks of the gospels. As I did so, I noticed how little Jesus talked about having our sins forgiven so that we could get into heaven when we die, even though that was really the whole of the picture I had been given. I also noticed how often Jesus talks about life. Particularly in John's gospel and letters, life is all over the place.

For example:

- "The Son gives life to whomever he wishes."[15]
- "Anyone who hears my word...has passed over from death to life."[16]
- "The bread that I will give for the life of the world is my flesh."[17]
- "Whoever has the Son has life; whoever does not have the Son of God does not have life."[18]

Those are just a few of the many instances in which we can notice how "life" and "salvation" could even be substituted for one another here, and make good sense. Perhaps you may want to pause your reading of this book and read through the gospel of John, or 1 John, being attentive to this salvation-life connection.

Three

FAITH

For God alone my soul waits in silence;
from him comes my salvation....
Trust in him at all times, O people;
pour out your heart before him;
God is a refuge for us.
Psalm 62:1,8

Let all those who are real members of the Church, see that they walk holy and
*unblamable in all things....Show them your **faith** by your works.*[19]
John Wesley

No one will follow Jesus who has to hesitate before saying, "Jesus is smart."[20]
Dallas Willard

NOT ONLY ARE THE PECANS FROM MY DAD'S ORCHARD tasty, but I also appreciate how they look. If you were here with me right now, I would pridefully point out how the pecans you find in your grocery store are shriveled and brown, but these Harris pecans come out of their shell plump and full, with a great golden-yellow color. Plus, the pecans don't even have to come out of their shells to look nice. The shells themselves, when they come off of a tree rather than a store shelf, have very distinct markings and shapes. It is not unusual for me to have at least a few pecans in my backpack at any time, as I'm always ready to point these features out to someone. (Someday, someone will approach and ask me,

"Would you happen to be carrying any pecans in that backpack?", and then I'll finally have my chance).

Even if I eventually do get that opportunity to put a few beautiful shells on display for someone, there is an obvious difference between the pecans in my backpack and the ones that are in this process we have described of being delivered into full life: the pecans I carry around with me are not in the ground. They are not in the conditions for their growth. If grace is the gift that grows the seed, these seeds are completely missing out on the gift.

Here's a place where my metaphor runs into a limit. These pecans which I may have in my backpack on any given day did not have a choice about whether or not to go into the soil and remain in the conditions for their growth. So if we are going to say that you and I are the seeds, to make that work, we have to emphasize that we may be nuts, but we aren't just nuts—we are nuts with choices.

So, imagine with me a little pecan that could make its own choices. For the sake of writing this chapter, let's give him a name: since he's from the Harris pecan orchard, we'll call him Harry. If he has choices, how hard do you think it would it be for little Harry to choose to leave himself there in the dirt in my dad's orchard? Remember, this is a pecan with options, so he could be out doing all kinds of things. Surely a pecan with choices could get on some TV shows, or at least make some good commercials. Harry can easily come up with a long list of options for things he could be doing in order to make a life for himself, and you know, I wouldn't really blame him for trying.

But if this pecan-with-choices goes out and exercises all of his power of choice in order to broaden his experiences and to do all kinds of things, then—wherever in the world Harry is doing those things and whatever in the world is happening with him, what won't be happening is cooperation with grace, because little Harry has separated himself from the conditions conducive to his growth and salvation. As Harry goes about, trying to secure his own happiness, he will not be in the process of being grown into what he really is. On that path, Harry will never know a pecan life to its fullest, the kind of life that is available to him, as he could become truly and fully what he is in all of his pecan-ness.

The good news is that Harry never totally gets away from grace. Even if he is out galavanting in a distant country, he will still occasionally become aware of the constraints of his shell, and feel a draw toward being planted. But if, as he feels that draw, he chooses to let himself be distracted rather than give himself over to it, he may never realize the growing gap between the limits of his hard shell and what he could have been becoming if he had chosen to leave himself in the dirt. How different Harry's life is when he is separated from the gift that grows him.

————

How do we separate ourselves from God's grace? If grace is as abundantly available as the Scriptures insist, then—practically—how do we refuse it? *If grace is the gift that grows us, we refuse it when we don't let ourselves stay planted in the conditions conducive to our growth.*

You may remember the passage in the Sermon on the Mount when Jesus tells us not to worry. He says, look at the birds of the air…look at the lilies of the field, they don't have to worry about the things they need. Our heavenly Father takes care of them, and, Jesus says, guess what: God cares more about you, his children, than he does about birds or lilies. So seek first his kingdom and righteousness, and everything you need will be given to you.

It's a familiar passage, but there's one little phrase in it which I often overlooked. E. Stanley Jones comments on this, as Jesus says, "consider the lilies, *how they grow*…." That's the same issue we are considering in this chapter, and in this book, and really in any of the more reflective moments in our lives. If grace is here, and grace is God's gift that grows us, and we consider *how* the lilies or the pecans grow, what do we learn?

Jesus says about the lilies: "They neither toil nor spin." I think we could also add that neither do they get tense and anxious about their own growth, taking it into their own hands, convinced that they know how to pursue their own happiness better than God does. No, we understand that lilies and pecan trees grow naturally.

Jones describes it well:

The plant grows by receptivity to earth and air and sun. It learns how to take, to receive. It keeps the channels of receptivity open, and the earth and the sun do the rest. This is the secret Jesus is teaching us through the lilies—"how they grow." When we learn that, we have learned the most important lesson life has to teach us. Without it life is a fight—a fight from your own center, with your own resources, and the end is tense exhaustion. With it you fight the good fight of faith from God as the center, with His resources, and the end is triumphant exhilaration. [21]

Ruth Haley Barton describes the same characteristic of the spiritual life:

In the end, this is the most hopeful thing any of us can say about spiritual transformation: I cannot transform myself, or anyone else for that matter. What I can do is create the conditions in which spiritual transformation can take place, by developing and maintaining a rhythm of spiritual practices that keep me open and available to God. [22]

That is how the lilies and pecans grow, and it's how you and I grow: we *stay* in "the conditions…that keep us open and available to God." In fact, it is all that we do. It can, and will, take a lifetime of effort on our part. In what seems like a paradox, it requires much effort and yet we are utterly powerless to make ourselves grow in any measure. We cannot force any more love, joy, or peace into our lives. Thankfully, though, just as there are natural processes in place in nature that have allowed fifty-three acres of pecan trees to grow in the desert of west Texas, God's grace is dependably and generously available to work in us. Our part is to keep those "channels of receptivity" open.

———

Harry, our pecan that can choose, can opt to go jaunting around the world, taking the project of his own happiness into its own hands (if he had hands), rather than staying planted, and remaining in the conditions conducive to grace. (Of course, the Harry that is you and me has done that very thing a thousand times. We have resisted God's grace—usually not so much by choosing some blatant sin over the love of God, but most often simply by not staying planted, by closing off those channels of receptivity.) Well, why does Harry do it? Why would he choose to become the prodigal pecan?

Ultimately, *he doesn't really **trust** the farmer*. Harry thinks that fully entrusting himself to the farmer and his intentions and competencies really won't work out as well for him as some of the other options he has in mind.

Harry is a good pecan. I think it hurt his feelings when I called him the prodigal pecan a minute ago, because in actuality he has never gone off and done all of that kind of wild stuff that comes to mind with the word prodigal. No, he consistently returns to his hole in the soil. Every Sunday morning, he comes and sits in it for a while. He can spend a lot of time around that hole in the soil—maybe even teach some classes or lead some retreats telling others how good it is to be in the soil. He may even get a job working around the farm, because of his devotion to pecans being in the soil.

But all of those things are very, very different processes from staying planted, keeping those channels of receptivity open, and remaining there long enough for God's grace to do its profoundly good and generous work of growing our seed into what it truly is. All of those things are very different from our seed really *entrusting* itself to the farmer, trusting that the farmer is good, and that the farmer is able.

———

The word which the Bible most often uses for that kind of trust is *faith*. If we have often reduced grace and salvation to having to do with forgiving acceptance, then we have also often reduced faith to having to do with believing the right stuff about God. Essentially, we think of faith as meaning we can say "I agree" to everything in the Apostles' Creed, which can still leave faith out of contact with the large majority of our daily lives.

As deeply important as those creeds are, assenting to what they say is a long, long way from entrusting ourselves to a person. If grace (God's gift that grows us) is the central, generously given ingredient in God's work of salvation (our deliverance into full life), then *faith is entrusting ourselves to God*, allowing ourselves to stay planted long enough for grace to take its effect over time.

So if Harry were really to trust his farmer and stay planted in the conditions conducive to grace, it would mean that he would have to trust that the kind of life into which the farmer would lead him is indeed the absolute best kind of life for him. It may well be very different from the kind of life which Harry has known to this point, yet at the same time—it's still really, truly, authentically the kind of life for which he was made.

Harry would have to trust that it's okay for the process to be slow. Grace grows the seed at the rate in which grace grows the seed, and though some pretty substantial changes are always happening, it isn't very fast. There are no microwave pecan orchards. Or, as I once heard Eugene Peterson say, "there are no steroids in matters of holiness."[23] If we stay planted, keeping those channels of receptivity open, sometimes all it feels like is that the seed is going into the ground and *dying*, rather than being grown by grace into a great tree in the midst of a great orchard. Indeed, that feeling of a dying process is no illusion,

> *Sometimes all it feels like is that the seed is going into the ground and dying, rather than being grown by grace into a great tree in the midst of a great orchard.*

but is what is happening to the seed as it stays there in the ground awaiting any kind of new life to emerge.

Then even after a lot of waiting, when something sprouts up, it will probably be about seven years before Harry is ever going to see a pecan on his branches. Those will likely be seven years of wondering what's wrong with himself and comparing himself to other trees that appear to be doing much better than he is. But grace will do its work—over time—and entrusting himself to the farmer means that our beloved Harry will have to abandon the outcomes of his own existence to God.

Each year in my church around New Year's Day, we use a prayer called the Wesleyan Covenant Prayer, which includes lines like these: "Lord, let me be employed for thee or laid aside for thee, let me be full, let me be empty, exalted for thee or brought low for thee, let me have all things, let me have nothing."[24] That's a prayer of entrusting ourselves to God in the way required for us to stay planted for the long haul, and I imagine that Harry would find it needful to have a prayer like that committed to memory.

Teilhard de Chardin has a poem called "Patient Trust" that starts with a great first line: "Above all, trust in the slow work of God." (Or, we could reword that in our language for this book: "Above all, trust in slow grace.")

The poem goes on to say:

Above all, trust in the slow work of God.

We are quite naturally impatient in everything
to reach the end without delay.
We should like to skip the intermediate stages.
We are impatient of being on the way to something
unknown, something new.
And yet it is the law of all progress
that it is made by passing through
some stages of instability —
and that it may take a very long time.

And so I think it is with you...[25]

If Harry is going to entrust himself to his farmer in that way, he also has to trust that there's more going on than can be seen. Not just can the process be slow, but the majority of the processes of grace's work are invisible—often even unfelt. So Harry, you, and I cannot stay planted unless we deeply trust this farmer. Maybe another way of rewording "Above all, trust in the slow work of God," could be to say, "Trust God, and trust the process." Harry won't see all that's happening to him by grace because so much of the work of the gift that grows him happens underground, where no one sees it—not even him. But if he lives in that way of abandoning the outcomes of his own life to the farmer, because of his deep trust, then going a while without seeing anything happening is okay. Then, we can pray a prayer like "Let me be full, let me be empty, let me have all things, let me have nothing" with heartfelt sincerity, because we have come to trust in this person, God, more than we've come to trust in the potential happiness we thought any of those outcomes might be able to bring us.

Let's go back to our house. Again, I don't mind being a bit repetitive here, but I'll emphasize some different things this time to help us make some connections as we transition from Part One (our beliefs) to Part Two (our practices).

My life without God is like an old house where no one has lived for decades, all boarded up and dark on the inside. The house is pretty useless without light; it was intended to be lit up. Its structure is still sound, but for whatever reason, no one lives there and so all of the windows and doors have been boarded up and no light has been allowed in.

God's grace is like the sunlight that is all around the house. It has been there every day, available to penetrate the house's darkness, but blocked out because there is no life in the house and barriers have been built up to keep out intruders, animals, rocks from the neighborhood boys, and also consequentially, the light.

If my soul is the darkened house and God's grace is the light that empowers life in that house, then these practices, these means of grace, are the windows which, if unboarded, will be the channels through which God's light comes into my darkened house. Reflection on Scripture opens one window and those first rays of light instantly overpower the darkness. Then getting enough rest opens another, then fasting, then prayer, then confession, then margin, then communion, then service, and eventually—as I learn to do those things in ways that open me to God's grace, God's light so fills that house that the darkness has been driven out from every room, and it is again a house suitable for life.

Maybe it would be better to speak of these practices, these means of grace, as being the *act* of unboarding the windows rather than being the windows themselves, for these means of grace are necessarily things that we *do*. These actions are the effort we put into the process. God's lavish, loving, generous grace is always available and it's around long before we realize it, and we are not passive in the process of its coming into our lives to heal all of the formerly sin-sickened places in our world and replace them with Jesus' abundant, thriving life.

Looking at our practices in terms of them being means of God's grace into our lives helps us to make sense of a few helpful and important things. Think of the conversation that happens in a lot of ways, even within the New Testament itself, about the apparent tension between faith and works. Paul says that it is by grace we are saved through faith, which necessarily means that it isn't dependent on what we do. Then James comes back and says, show me a faith that doesn't do anything, and I'll show you a faith that's dead.

Hopefully Harry helps us to see that they are both right in very important ways. Our trust in God does not consist of doing things. The trust which enables my wife and me to open ourselves to one another in our life together rather than closing ourselves off from each other is about my trust in her as a person, and hers in me. Yet also, if we trust, we naturally do things according to that trust. If we trust God, we open ourselves to God. If we trust God, we open ourselves to the grace that grows us. If we trust God, then by that trust—by *faith*—we practice these means of grace.

There's an important passage in this regard near the end of 1 Corinthians. In chapter fifteen, Paul is setting up a great passage about the resurrection, and he starts out by referring to his past, how he had been a persecutor of Christians. Then he says this:

> *But by the grace of God I am what I am, and his grace toward me has not been in vain. On the contrary, I worked harder than any of them—though it was not I, but the grace of God that is with me.* [26]

Paul is recognizing that he was changed from being the seed to being the tree, and the only way it happened was by God's gift of grace. God's grace grew him. God's grace delivered him from what he previously was into life—into being fully and truly who he was in Christ. As he says it here,

God's grace toward him was not in vain. He kept the channels of receptivity open. He practiced the means of grace, cooperating with grace by the effort he put into the process: "I worked harder than any of them, but it wasn't me. It was the grace of God that is with me."

If you and I want to experience what it's like for God's grace to take its full effect upon us, we have to get in touch with our desire for God. We will not be able to entrust ourselves to God to the level that Paul describes unless we first wrestle with how deeply we *want* God. Do we really want God more than any of the options we have in mind each day for securing our own happiness? Once we pay attention to it, our desire for God draws us to trust God in all of the ways that we've described in our adventures with Harry, and that trust in God *is* faith.

Although Paul didn't use the word *faith* in the passage quoted above, he could not live as he described without a deep trust in God, so it's a description by someone who has faith— someone who knows what it's like to entrust himself to God, to leave himself planted in the conditions conducive to his growth.

Two other statements of trust in God have been very helpful to me, and I hope that by this point we have sufficient context for understanding them. Wesley says, "Stir up the spark of grace which is now in you, and [God] will give you more grace."[27] And Willard says that grace is opposed to earning, not to effort.[28]

Perhaps in light of the statement from Saint Paul, and this one from John Wesley, we might be able to modify Willard's statement and say, "Grace is opposed to earning, not to effort, and in fact grace flourishes when we cooperate with it through our trust in God."

———

Practice

Entrusting ourselves to God can feel like a really huge topic. We are about to turn the corner into looking at practical ways that we can do so as habits in our lives, but the actions that enflesh our trust in God don't have to be complex. Most of us, if we put ourselves in prodigal Harry's shoes (if he had feet) could think of at least one practical and doable thing we could do *today* based on our desire for and trust in God.

As mentioned in an earlier chapter, one of the most important aspects of our coming to a genuine trust in God is to trust that God loves us exactly as we are. So, rather than having to come up with anything that feels more religious, perhaps a step to take in trust today could be to consider the question, "What is something I could do to enjoy the reality of God's love for me?"

When you have an idea (and perhaps you already do), don't distract yourself from it. Stay planted.

Part Two

PRACTICING GRACE

Four

PRAYER

*But now more than ever the word about Jesus spread abroad; many crowds would gather to hear him and to be cured of their diseases. But he would withdraw to deserted places and **pray**.*
Luke 5:16

First, all who desire the grace of God are to wait for it in the way of ***prayer***.[29]
John Wesley

Prayer *is nothing but a proper way for persons to interact*.[30]
Dallas Willard

Here is my guess at the biggest, most pervasive grace-obstruction in the lives of sincere Christians today: *distraction*. I have known very few people who ever intentionally decided that they wanted to be something other than truly and fully who they are in Christ, but I have never gone a single day without being around a distracted Christian. (This is true since—even though I've unconsciously tried to do so in the past—I never have figured out how to go a day without being around myself.)

Later in this chapter, we will give some attention to the distractions that barrage us *during* our times of prayer, but those are not the dangerous kind that I'm referring to here. Rather, the distractions that may be the biggest threat to our growth in grace are any of those innumerable forms that keep us from ever really incorporating these grace-full practices into our lifestyles. Even if I dabble in them from time to time, distraction may still exercise authority over my lifestyle by keeping my attention from the depths of my desire for God and the generous availability of God's grace in this present moment. This kind of distraction's danger is that it can keep me pseudo-satisfied by occasionally allowing me to dip my toes into life with God while keeping me from ever plunging in and swimming in it. To modify and combine Wesley's and Paul's words, these distractions keep me from stirring the spark of grace that is already in me, and therefore limit the effect that grace will have on me. In other words, the problem is not the distractions that inevitably come into my mind *when* I pray, but the ones that are so ingrained in my habits that they keep me from praying.

> *The primary problem is not the distractions that inevitably come into my mind when I pray, but the ones that are so ingrained in my habits that they keep me from praying.*

Several years ago when I was working on a book called *Live Prayerfully: How Ordinary Lives Become Prayerful*, I bummed some free editing help from my cousin. She's a perceptive woman, and right from the book's Introduction, she asked me a simple and important question that has stuck with me since that time: "What do you really mean by *prayerful*?" When she asked me, I was very ready to be done with the book, and I probably didn't give sufficient thought to be able to offer a meaningful response which could have added clarity to what I was trying to say.

Now, however, I think I can identify a simple and satisfactory description of a prayerful life: one in which I live attentively to God. There are going to be specific practices that are part of any such life (examples of which we will explore in the majority of this chapter), but that characteristic of attentiveness to God is the essence of my desire to live prayerfully.

Psalm 27 describes the prayerful attitude of someone who has learned to deal with the distractions and lean into their desire to live attentively to God:

> *One thing I asked of the LORD,*
> *   that will I seek after:*
> *to live in the house of the LORD*
> *   all the days of my life,*
> *to behold the beauty of the LORD,*
> *   and to inquire in his temple.*

I want that kind of prayerful life—experiencing my normal and abnormal days while being attentive to God, beginning and ending each day aware of that attentiveness to God as the one thing I am seeking. When I let the dust settle that gets worked up in the activity of everyday life, I can feel a bit more deeply the extent to which I desire that life, and grace enables me to progressively arrange my days accordingly. While busyness is a critical issue here, it is not the only factor. I can have a very full day, or a very laid-back day, and my wants can still be pulled in a hundred directions. Or I can be very aware throughout the same kind of full day or relaxed day that everything I genuinely, deeply desire is available right here and right now because of God's love, presence, and generosity. I have the sense that this is the tip of the iceberg of what is meant by familiar phrases like Soren Kierkegaard's, "Purity of heart is to will one thing,"[31] or David's "The LORD is my shepherd, I shall not be in want,"[32] or Paul's statement that God's grace was sufficient for him.[33]

Much of our ability to live attentively rather than being blinded by distractions is dependent on putting habits in place in our lives that give us opportunities to repeatedly return our attention to God. In our seed metaphor, it can be as if we made the decision to stay planted for the long term and allow grace to do its work, but we still sleepwalk out of that hole where our new lives are being given to us. We need rhythms of waking up, going back home, returning our attention to God, and resuming the cooperation with grace.

James Bryan Smith describes these daily rhythms:

Just like the fire in the fireplace, I need to stoke the fire throughout the day. I do this by pausing for short times of prayer every hour or two, by reading the Scriptures or spending a few moments reading a devotional book....These are the logs that I add to the existing fire to keep it burning brightly....I don't do all of these things because I want God to love me and bless me, nor to avoid punishment or impress people with my piety. I do all of this to keep the fire burning. I do them because I am spiritually weak. I cannot maintain an effective and joyful Christian life without these activities. [34]

In the context of Smith's words, he is describing a different set of practices than the specific ones we are about to explore, but the goal he is seeking is the same. The essence of a prayerful life is attentiveness to God, not the prayer practices themselves. The practices are the means, not the end. They are ways that we exercise our faith, leave ourselves planted, put another log on the fire, and cooperate with grace. Their purpose is—over time—to allow God's grace to grow us into being fully and truly who we are in Christ.

We will explore a framework for rhythms of prayer in the rest of the chapter (which is also described more fully in *Live Prayerfully*). As we look into these three practices (which are praying with other people's words, praying without words, and praying with your own words), I find it helpful to think of them in terms of majors and minors. If you feel particularly drawn to one of these ways of praying as you read and have the sense that practicing it could be a very life-giving channel of God's grace for you at this point in your life, I encourage you to let it be your major for at least six months. Let yourself really lean into it. You don't need a different life than the one you've been given to be able to live prayerfully—you already have all of the grace and permission that you need. (The minors are important too, but we'll come back to them at the end of the chapter.)

Praying With Other People's Words

Jesus' disciples wanted to learn his way of praying, which is natural for followers of a rabbi. They saw him pray, asked for guidance in how they could learn to do as he did, and he responded to them by teaching them a prayer:

> *Once Jesus was praying in a particular place. When he had finished, one of his disciples approached. "Teach us to pray, Master," he said, "just like John taught his disciples."*
>
> *"When you pray," replied Jesus, "this is what to say:...*
>
> *Father, may your name be honored; may your kingdom come; give us each day our daily bread; and forgive us our sins, since we too forgive all our debtors; and don't put us to the test."*[35]

Both Jesus and those disciples also prayed in ways other than using the words of this prayer, but we miss something if we skip the fact that Jesus taught his apprentices to *recite* this prayer, and that the early Christians took on the habit of doing so. Even the earliest generations of Christians were taught to pray these words of Jesus' model prayer three times per day.[36]

Think what it would be like to develop a habit of engaging in this ancient practice of praying the words of the Lord's Prayer three times per day by imagining yourself ten years from now with this habit. Do you see your life being more grace-full? Can you see how this simple rhythm of methodically returning your attention to God throughout your days, weeks, months, and years, could open space for an attentive, prayerful life to develop?

———

Let's say that you and I are part of a small cluster of young saplings, who have been planted in this pecan orchard and have committed ourselves to supporting one another in this long process of being grown by grace into being fully and truly who we are. What if, when we look across the orchard where we are planted, we not only see other trees about our size, but we also see some beautiful, old, strong, long-fruitful trees? We would naturally want to learn how grace grew them. We would want to listen to their stories and emulate the ways they have cooperated with grace through their lives.

I can easily imagine the disciples as the young saplings who had observed Jesus—the strong fruitful tree—when they approached him with their request, "Teach us to pray."

Because those early Christians lived in much closer proximity to Christianity's Jewish roots than most of us do, developing the practice of praying Jesus' prayer three times daily would have had a familiar feel to them since the prayer practices of their communities were structured around praying the psalms and other prayers at set times each day. So, if we were to look across the orchard, notice some of the old-timers who learned from Jesus and his early followers how to pray, and offer the same request, "Teach us to pray," we might notice some glaring differences between the rhythms of prayer in which they were formed in their communities and the ways that most of us pray.

First—again—there's the rhythm of it. Unless you are a part of a monastic community, today it's uncommon that the daily rhythms of prayer which have been central to the formation of so many of God's people through the centuries would be a central component of your daily routines. While I don't know anyone who isn't a monk who structures the schedule of their day around Psalm 119's "seven times a day I praise you," I do know people and communities who have found two, three, or four scheduled but brief prayerful pauses per day to be an important means of allowing grace to regularly return our attention to God, giving us space to entrust ourselves to God again.

Another glaring difference would be the primary source of what they prayed at those set times of the day: the psalms. We would quickly note how central the psalms have been in the prayer practices of those mature trees versus how little the majority of us have learned to open ourselves to God's grace through them. As I have sought to stay enrolled in the psalms' school of prayer in recent years, I have been struck by my own lack of ability to be as gut-wrenchingly honest in my prayers as is evident throughout the psalms. My prayers often lack both the expressions of desperation and of exuberant joy which we confront when we seek to join millennia of God's people in praying these words. Of course it isn't that I ever knowingly try to be dishonest in my prayers, but part of what the psalms teach us is that to live attentively to God, we also have to learn to live attentively to ourselves and the world around us, and then to weave each of those threads together each time we return our attention to God in prayer.

Even as I write this, I've just seen yet another headline about a terrorist attack ending the lives of people today, and I am again reminded of how much I want to be shaped by the psalms. When my "teach me to pray" request leads me to the psalms again this evening, it's possible that I might skim over the words on the page and then get on to the rest of what I had planned, but I hope not. I hope that the words there will help me to connect the realities of this life I've been given—that I will be able to entrust to God my own experiences of the day, the anguish and the joy of those I contact in personal conversation or through the distance of a news headline.

Perhaps another reminder is in order that even if we develop the best habits of praying the best words at the best times of each day, these practices of praying other people's words can be accepted as means of God's grace that grows us, or they can be twisted into grace-obstructions (as in my

Christmas morning story from an earlier chapter). But even when that is the case, the problem is not the practice itself. Instead, we have now moved into dealing with a different kind of distraction than we discussed to open this chapter. When our prayer practices turn into something other than means of God's grace into our lives, we may keep practicing, but we are not living as attentively as we might. This kind of distraction is usually running in the background of our minds, but Christians through the centuries have commended another way of praying which brings them to the forefront, which is to pray without relying on any words at all.

Praying Without Words

This issue of distractions during our times of prayer is an important dynamic regardless of which way of praying we may be engaging in, but it inevitably comes to the fore when we seek to follow the lead of so many followers of Christ who have found unique grace in habits of praying without words.

When I first became a father, one of my favorite things to do in the evenings was to go on walks around our neighborhood pushing my kids' stroller. The habit started before my son had turned one year old. It was amazing how quickly all could become well in his little world if we put him in his stroller and went for a walk, regardless of how fussy he may have been in the house.

I loved watching his reactions during the walks when he was that age, as he was just beginning to wake up to the world around him. It was a delight to me to watch his fascination when he would see a cat sitting under a car, hear a dog barking, see other neighborhood children out playing, or even just how he would be mesmerized by leaning his head over the side of the stroller and watching the pavement pass by underneath.

My favorite part, though, was at the end of the walks. I would push the stroller back into our driveway, and walk back around in front of him to open our garage door. When he saw me, he would get a very surprised, wide-eyed expression on his face that seemed to say, "What? *You* were here?"

He had been so wrapped up in the things he saw in the world around him that he felt like he was just out for a drive alone in his stroller. He had completely forgotten that I was there with him, even though all along I was in the place I needed to be to give us the opportunity to have the walk together.

Those memories came back to me in a much-needed way during that same period of my life, when I was attending a Transforming Community retreat focused on silence and solitude. I was very eager to grow into a life more attentive to God than I had been living, so I was soaking up the rich teaching on practical ways to do so. I was walking back to the retreat house from the building where our teaching sessions were held. After following a path through the woods, the path ended at a road which extended in both directions. It was at this point that I wished I had paid better attention to some of the instructions our retreat leaders had given. All I could remember at that moment was that they had said something about if we encountered such a spot and went one direction, the walk back to the retreat house would be short and easy; if I went the other direction, I would still get back to the retreat house, but only after a three and one-half mile walk around a lake. I made my best guess as to the correct direction. About thirty minutes later, my tired legs let me know unmistakably that I had gone the wrong way.

Initially, I was okay with my error and decided to make the best of it, as it gave me the opportunity to get some much-needed exercise and savor the scenery of the lake. I enjoyed doing so for a few minutes, but then gave in to frustration. My thoughts quickly turned to how I had been looking forward to a restful, relaxing time of quiet with God in my comfortable room during the hours that we had been given for solitude. At that point, although I knew that prayer was still possible during my walk, I still had two unchosen miles remaining ahead of me and the reality of the impending exercise wasn't quite as appealing as the thought of it had been.

I spent most of the remainder of the walk pouting because my backpack felt heavy, my legs were beginning to throb, and I wasn't able to spend time with God like I had wanted to. I had an occasional burst of spiritual motivation and decided to try to practice some of the prayer exercises I had just been taught, but quickly became distracted by the scenery, walking past other people, and just getting lost in my own thoughts.

Finally, I made it back to the retreat house very tired and ready to get to my room. As I walked through the parking lot up to our building, it was as if I was the little boy in the stroller who was surprised to see my daddy walk around in front of me, realizing that—regardless of how I had felt—I had never been alone on that walk.

I realized the similarities between the things that caught my son's eye on the walks in our neighborhood and the things that occupied my attention as I walked around that lake. From the child's perspective, I realized that I, too, had been so wrapped up in the things I saw in the world around me that I had felt like I was just out for a stroll all alone, and had completely forgotten that God was there with me, though nothing had ever been done to hide God's presence from me. In fact, the world around me wasn't the enemy—what I really wanted was to be able to enjoy the scenery and sounds while also being attentive to the unseen one who was with me.

From the parent's perspective, I thought about how much I enjoyed watching my little boy engage his world even though he had forgotten that I was there with him very early into our walks. My knowledge that he was enjoying the world around him to the point that he had forgotten about my company in no way diminished my enjoyment of our walks, because his level of awareness of my presence was appropriate to his maturity and I trusted that he was growing and developing.

Once I woke up to the fact that God had been on the walk all along, I also realized the silliness of being disappointed in not spending time with God in the way I had planned. God's presence with me on the walk was no less real than it would have been if I had turned the other way on the road and gone directly back to my room. It was as if my son would have passed some of the time on his walk being concerned about strolling by himself rather than spending time with his daddy as he had planned. It would have been both humorous and sad if, while I was accompanying him and giving him my constant attention, he had any thoughts such as, "I really wanted to be playing in my room with my Daddy right now, but instead I am out here all by myself riding in this stroller." Yet that is precisely the silliness that characterized my disappointment on the walk around the lake over not being able to spend time with God in the way that I had intended. I do believe it is good to make plans for and anticipate times with God, but I have also now been taught that those wide-eyed moments of realization that God has already been here are just as delightful, both to God and to us.

Seven years after turning the wrong way on that road, my son and I still go on walks around our neighborhood. He no longer rides in a stroller, but walks next to me, sometimes holding my hand and talking to me about the things that catch his attention. Also, I have returned for several more retreats to the lake where I turned the wrong way, and I now prefer to take the long route back to the retreat house. I hope that with every opportunity to take that long walk around the lake, God will be able to notice small ways in which, like my son, I am gradually becoming more aware of my Father's presence with me in the midst of the world God delights to watch me enjoy.

———

Becoming more aware of the already-reality of God's presence with us is the core of the grace we seek in developing a practice of praying without words. Yet as rich as that awareness is when it grows, this way of praying is one that presents significant challenges. None of us will stay planted in it long enough for it to take effect unless we pay attention to the wisdom passed down to us from previous folks whose desire for God led them to explore this frontier.

A primary mark on the map that they have handed down to us is that it won't take venturing very far into this kind of prayer before we encounter our distractions. The distractions seem like formidable enough foes that if we aren't paying attention to the guidance of those gone before us, we will feel like the majority of the Israelite spies sent into Canaan, who returned and reported back to Moses, "they are stronger than we are," describing themselves as grasshoppers in comparison to those they encountered.[37]

At this point in my life, I am still not one who has navigated all of the territory, handing down reliable maps for others to follow. But I am one who has crossed over the border, and its fruit is indeed good enough that I want to learn how to take up residence here. That's why I am immensely grateful for the Calebs and Joshuas who have gone before me, seen the inhabitants of the land, and come back to report, "the Lord is with us. Do not be afraid of them."

The value of having the guidance of those gone before us is that we are assured that this exploration of praying in ways where we are seeking to do nothing except be with God is not going to be obstacle-free. They teach us to not only be unafraid of things like distractions (and another major marker on their map: boredom), but that they are to be expected. Not only can we expect them, but the challenges that have been marked for us are transformed from threats we feel like we need to avoid, to instead being invaluable indicators that we are following the intended path.[38]

Our mental distractions when we want to eliminate all of the noise and just be with God seem like such pesky problems to us. The point, however, is for us to be with God as simply and as often as we can, so that our awareness of God's indwelling presence with us in the entirety of our lives is given a chance to grow and bring us life.

Saint Augustine gives us a very helpful image along these lines. He is describing Sabbath rest, rather than specifically prayer without words, but the mental distractions are the same. He says that it's as if we have heard the invitation to "be still, and know that I am God," but then find ourselves surrounded by a swarm of gnats. "They are back as soon as you drive them off. Just like the futile fantasies that swarm in our minds."[39]

When I have an image like that written on the map from someone farther along than I am, it helps me to be encouraged because although the gnats are indeed pesky, they aren't intimidating enough to cause me to turn back. Instead, it's easy for me to picture myself being with God while still flustered by the gnat swarm around me. But God is still there, looking at me lovingly, and very glad I responded to the gracious invitation to come and be together. For the time being, these gnat-distractions are an indication that I'm making the same worthwhile exploration that Augustine and countless others have made ahead of me. My hope is that over the months, years, and decades of staying here and showing up to be loved by God by being together without words, fewer and fewer gnats will swarm around me, and even when they do, my attention will go more naturally through them to God.[40]

Praying With Your Own Words

If living attentively to God is the essence of a prayerful life, one of the simple but profound discoveries we may make along the way is of God's attentiveness to us. Any time we feel our love for God, we discover that it did not start with us, but is part of the gift of God's love for us. Each time that we are aware of our desire to experience more fullness in our life with God, it is a reminder of the inseparability of our lives from God, that it really is "in him that we live, move and have our being."[41]

One way of describing this discovery is to say that we find that the purpose of our existence is not to appease God, nor to obey God, nor ultimately even to serve God. Rather, as we get more tastes of what Jesus meant when he said, "abide in me, and I will abide in you,"[42] we discover the simple yet mind-blowing dynamic of Christianity: our lives are meant to be shared with God's.

Dallas Willard's description of prayer points at this, saying that prayer is talking with God about what we are doing together.[43] So, as helpful as it can be to learn the ancient rhythms of praying the psalms and the Lord's prayer at set times each day, and as much space for grace as is created when I develop habits of being with God without words, as I discover more of what it's like to live in dependence on God's life in me, I will inevitably have times of talking with God in my own words about this life we are sharing.

One simple framework for praying with my own words in a way that increases my attentiveness to God over time is to practice reviewing my day with God. I've found that I need a few times per week when I look back over the previous twenty-four to forty-eight hours, considering questions like:

- When was I aware of God during the day, and when was I distracted?
- When did I have a sense of being open to God, to those around me, to what was going on in myself, and to the

world in which I live, and when was I closed in each of those areas?

- In what ways was I seeking to seize control of my own life, and in what ways was I able to entrust the outcomes of my life to God?
- When was I receiving my life as a gift, keeping those channels of receptivity open? And when was I working too hard strategizing for my own happiness?

> *A prayer of review often gives me a second chance to live a moment with God which I missed at the time.*

Often when praying in this way, it is as if I am given a second chance to live a moment with God which I missed at the time. Perhaps I recall an instance of looking into my wife's eyes, or of enjoying the weather, or of feeling engaged in meaningful work, but I kept moving through the day without really feeling the significance of it. This prayer of review gives me the chance to go back and express my deep gratitude for those moments before they vanish from my memory.

Other times I recall moments that I regret from the day, and it is an opportunity to view those with God as well, resting in the assurance of being loved and invited into this life because of God's love for me. I might recall a moment when I took out frustrations from some unrelated situation on my kids, or when I slipped into a feeling of needing to get my way and was highly irritable with anyone who proved to be an obstacle, or when I was dominated by anger, fear, greed, lust, or pride. When I review those moments with God, I find that God is consistently a patient, loving teacher, parent, and friend, and often I am able to see something that was going on under the surface of my awareness at the time which caused those reactions to come to the surface. Then I have the chance to ask for God's help and express my deep gratitude for God's love and forgiveness before I move into another day.[44]

Majors and Minors

I hope that you may feel drawn to one of these ways of praying, perhaps having the sense of being invited to it within the life you've been given and that doing so could deepen your attentiveness to God throughout each day. As mentioned earlier, you might find it helpful to consider one way as your "major" for some time, arranging your schedule around your desire to be with God in that way. When we do so, we can discover joy and freedom in being able to be with God in ways that we find to be very life-giving and conducive to the work of grace in us.

But it isn't only the majors that God uses as means of grace. If I am in a season of my life when my enjoyable major is to focus on praying the psalms and the Lord's Prayer at set times each day, while praying without words and with my own words hold less excitement for me, I tend to find the most cooperation with grace when I give the most attention to that major, but within a week also give some smaller attention to the minors (in this example, praying without words and with my own).

Each of these kinds of prayer is a means of grace, and each of them opens us to grace in a slightly different way. So as grace grows us, we will find that our desired major changes over time. That is appropriate as we are growing and changing, and we should feel the liberty to adjust our rhythms accordingly. Our practice of our major, however, will always be enhanced by not forgetting the minors and allowing grace to continue to grow us through them as well.

Practice

- Do you already have a sense of feeling drawn or invited to one of these ways of praying? Can you identify your major? If you cannot yet, don't let that worry you. Experiment with each way for some small period of time this week and see which one seems to stir the most hope or sense of freedom in you.

- When you have a major in mind, make some plans for how you would like to practice it within the realities of your lifestyle this week. Keep in mind that brief but regular times are often more valuable than lengthy experiments, because those are rhythms we will not be able to maintain. So, for example, how might you be able to practice your major for five minutes at least three or four times this week?

- As you let yourself explore your major, you might want to make use of one of the following resources:

Praying With Other People's Words:

- *A Pocket Guide to Prayer*, by Steve Harper, is a wonderful little guide for fixed-hour prayer guiding the reader through a month of prayer.

- Some readers get frustrated with the ways that prayer books often require flipping back and forth through the pages. *Live Prayerfully* contains a week of guides to prayer with no page-flipping necessary.

Praying Without Words:

- Take a walk with no goals other than to see and hear what is around you and to repeatedly return your attention to God.

- Consider reading Ruth Haley Barton's *Invitation to Solitude and Silence* as a simple yet profound guide. Each chapter contains a guided practice in solitude and silence.

- If you are particularly concerned with your distractions during prayer and how to deal with them, Martin Laird's *Into the Silent Land* offers very valuable wisdom.

Praying With Your Own Words:

- The website Pray-as-You-Go.org has a well-done selection of audio-guided prayers of review. Search their website for "examen" and listen to one of their recordings in the evening.
- Use one of the review questions I mentioned on p. 72 and write about it in a journal.

- After planning to enjoy your major, also consider when you could give five minutes in the week to each of the other two ways of praying (your minors). If you can get a week with a lot of your major, and a little of your minors, notice your attentiveness to God. Does it seem to be more deepened than with just your "favorite" way of praying?

Five

SCRIPTURE

The law of the LORD is perfect, reviving the soul;
the decrees of the LORD are sure, making wise the simple;
the precepts of the LORD are right, rejoicing the heart;
the commandment of the LORD is clear, enlightening the eyes;
the fear of the LORD is pure, enduring forever;
the ordinances of the LORD are true and righteous altogether.
More to be desired are they than gold, even much fine gold;
sweeter also than honey, and drippings of the honeycomb.
Psalm 19:7-10

Secondly. All who desire the grace of God are to wait for it
*in searching the **Scriptures**.*[45]
John Wesley

*To be a biblical Christian is not to have high views about the **Bible**. It is to*
*seek and know and live the life that is depicted in the **Bible**.*[46]
Dallas Willard

I live in the land of incredibly delicious Tex-Mex food. Having grown up on it (and it did its job as I was growing up eating it, since I'm 6'7"), one of the unforeseen losses I experienced when I moved away after high school was that the fajitas in other parts of the country never tasted right.

During the eleven years when I lived other places before moving back home to west Texas, any time my wife and I would return to visit my parents, I consumed as much precious Tex-Mex as possible. A week back at home would be split between my mom's great cooking and a couple of our favorite restaurants—particularly one called Rosa's Café and Tortilla Factory. I am neither proud nor ashamed to admit that during one week-long visit, I visited Rosa's five times. (The fajitas are that good.)

It is very appropriate that Rosa's includes "and Tortilla Factory" in its name, because the hot, freshly made tortillas are an essential part of the experience. They can be part of the tacos or burritos, or just eaten by themselves. (They're that good.) One of the best ways to eat them, though, is to spread some honey on them and turn them into a dessert.

I remember one particular meal there which gave me an image I may never forget. Lunchtime at Rosa's is usually crowded, so our table was close to that of the family next to us. A boy in that family, who looked to be about ten years old, had finished his meal and was pretty eager about his tortilla-and-honey dessert. However, for this boy, it was clear that the tortilla was a very secondary component of that recipe. His tortilla was saturated, permeated with honey. I think his parents may have been away from the table to get refills on their drinks when I looked over and saw him holding the tortilla up in the air, with honey running down his arm to his elbow. He couldn't help himself, and I enjoyed watching the boy sit there unaware of others around him, as he was licking his own arm, trying to get every last drop of honey that he could.

———

That image from Rosa's is a good match for how the psalmists apparently felt about their Scriptures:

"How sweet are your words to my taste,
sweeter than honey to my mouth!"[47]

"When I open my mouth I pant,
because I long for your commandments."[48]

"More to be desired are they than gold,
even much fine gold;
sweeter also than honey,
and drippings of the honeycomb."[49]

"Happy are those [whose]...
delight is in the law of the LORD,
and on his law they meditate day and night."[50]

There is quite a discrepancy between that boy's enjoyment of his tortilla and honey and the ways that I have often approached the Bible. I remember a point early in my years on staff at a church, around the time when I had begun digging in to great books on prayer. I was discovering authors like Richard Foster, Henri Nouwen and others, whose writings on prayer stirred me deeply, and I was beginning to experiment with ways that what they were describing could open me to God's grace (although I didn't have that language for it yet). I loved it and I was growing, but it hit me one day that something was a bit amiss. I found myself eager to read a book about prayer, but reading the Bible itself made me feel more like a nomad eating a mouthful of saltine crackers after walking without a drink through the desert than like a boy trying to lick honey off of his own elbow out of delight and desire. I could teach a lesson or preach a sermon from the Bible, but it was not my delight. I knew that wasn't particularly good, but it was honest.

The problem, of course, was not in the Bible, but in my approach to it. Honey itself can either be delicious or disgusting, depending on what we try to do with it. Honey as sweetener works significantly better than honey as soap. Similarly, there are numerous ways that we try to use the Bible which prevent it from being the inestimably valuable gift of

God's grace to us that the psalmists and so many others through the centuries have found it to be.

This becomes clear when we consider what parts of the Bible the "sweeter than honey" passages above would have been referring to (hint: it's books like Leviticus). I can put my head down and plow through reading those parts of the Old Testament, but I generally don't come away panting for more of them.

So how is that that the psalmists could open the book to those same passages of Scripture and come out saying that it's like honey and gold? I think part of the answer is that they approached the Scripture very differently than we normally do, and we will spend the rest of the chapter exploring ways to allow grace to close that gap, helping us to find the nourishment we need so desperately in the pages of the Bible.

Reading with the Heart

Of the three dynamics of reading that we will explore in this chapter, reading with the heart is the most challenging for me. Although I've been exploring it for more than a decade, I'm still nothing but a beginner at it. I don't think I'm alone in that. For many of us, this approach to the Bible is radically different from our normal habits.

When we talk about reading with our hearts, if that is going to do us any good, it needs to have a definite meaning for us. So, when I use the phrase, I'm indicating that we are exploring a way of reading that allows God's grace to reach a deep part of us, penetrating beyond our thoughts and our feelings and getting to our core—the very part of us that connects with God and sets the course of our lives.

This is challenging because it isn't just about opening the Bible, but about opening myself *to* the Bible, seeking ways of allowing the words of the Scripture to get as deeply into me as possible, shaping me, mastering me. This is a very different approach than simply seeking to get through a certain number of chapters on a regular basis. As Dallas Willard has indicated, the point is not to get me all the way through the Bible, but to get the Bible all of the way through me.[51]

To read the Bible without habits of allowing it to have access to those deeper parts of us is not just to miss the point, but is actually dangerous. As Eugene Peterson says, "an enormous amount of damage is done in the name of Christian living by bad Bible reading."[52]

John's gospel has a subsurface theme of contrasting Jesus, the living embodiment of the Word of God ("the Word became flesh") to others who read the Scriptures diligently but poorly. I think we can characterize them as not having read with the heart, and the results were damaging, as they missed the things that God was doing in front of them in and through Jesus. The important thing to note, for now, is that the damage was not caused by a *lack* of knowledge of the Scriptures. Rather, the ways they read their Scriptures ended up being twisted into something other than a means of grace, and therefore closed them off from what God was doing rather than helping them be open to it.

Perhaps the clearest statement of this theme is in John 5. Jesus was in a heated discussion with religious leaders, who were furious because he had healed a lame man on a Sabbath. Jesus said to them,

The Father who sent me has himself testified on my behalf. You have never heard his voice or seen his form, and you do not have his word abiding in you, because you do not believe him whom he has sent. You search the scriptures because you think that in them you have eternal life; and it is they that testify on my behalf. Yet you refuse to come to me to have life.[53]

This theme is evident repeatedly in John. People who knew their Scriptures better than the overwhelming majority of us (the present author included) were nonetheless completely blind to the fulfillment of those Scriptures that was taking place right in front of them.

Another example is in John 7. In conflict still stemming from Jesus healing the man on the Sabbath, it says:

> *On hearing his words, some of the people said, "Surely this man is the Prophet."*
>
> *Others said, "He is the Messiah."*
>
> *Still others asked, "How can the Messiah come from Galilee? Does not Scripture say that the Messiah will come from David's descendants and from Bethlehem, the town where David lived?" Thus the people were divided because of Jesus.*

For someone like me who is part of a tradition that places a lot of emphasis on sound biblical interpretation, these verses scream a warning: *They were right!* Jesus' opponents in this passage saw him through a lens of a correct interpretation of their Scriptures, which blinded them to who he was and what he was doing. They knew the facts in their Scriptures so well, and interpreted them accurately, and they still missed the Messiah standing right in front of them!

There are other times when John makes the point a bit more subtly, but these examples are enough to get the point across: knowledge of the Scriptures is wonderful (we certainly see an abundance of it displayed in the words of Jesus himself) but that knowledge without an openness of the heart can leave us in some very dangerous places—not only dangerous to ourselves, but in a place where we can do an enormous amount of harm to others and think we're being Scriptural in doing so. The history of Christianity is overflowing with lamentable examples of this.

We will get practical about this in a moment, but the point is important enough to underscore. Like a tool in the hands of a child who thinks it's a toy, the Bible often becomes something dangerous—distorted into a weapon for advancing our own agendas rather than being received as the centuries-long invitation of God to humanity to be reconciled and transformed. New Testament scholar Robert Mulholland, in his momentous book, *Shaped by the Word*, says that one of the dark sides of being a Bible-reading Christian is that we all seemingly have an

> *Like a tool in the hands of a child who thinks it's a toy, the Bible often becomes something dangerous—distorted into a weapon for advancing our own agendas rather than being received as the centuries-long invitation of God to humanity to be reconciled and transformed.*

"*ability to manipulate the scripture consciously or, more often, unconsciously to avoid a transforming encounter with God....We are often not looking for a transforming encounter with God. We are more often seeking some tidbits of information that will enhance our self-protective understanding of the Christian faith without challenging or confronting the way we live in the world.*"[54]

―――

So how do we avoid that trap and learn habits of opening the Bible while also being open to the Bible?

Above all else, we should keep in mind that it is a matter of *relationship* rather than of *technique*. Some methods of reading are more conducive to reading with the heart than others, but developing a habit of reading in those ways is not the same thing as learning to open myself to a person as I read. Reading with the heart is indeed a matter of the heart. When I come to read—regardless of the method I employ—am I, honestly, *willing* to be encountered by the living God? Am I submitting myself to God through the Scriptures, or am I the one in charge of this encounter? If particular guidance is given to me, do I trust God enough that I am already decided to keep following, or would I rather hear the invitation and then weigh my options?

So, whenever I read, I need to first find some way of coming as close as I can to taking my heart out of my chest, placing it on the open pages in front of me, and reiterating, "There, God, do with it whatever you will." Obviously—there are some limits involved in actually being able to do so, but that is the degree to which we are seeking to open ourselves to God through opening the Bible.

Once that orientation is in place, we can employ some of the useful methods of this kind of reading that have been commended to us from previous followers of Christ. The classic framework is called *lectio divina*. I will come back around to describing a version of it a bit more near the end of this chapter, but here is a brief description of the four movements of this method:

- *Read*: As you slowly and unhurriedly read a passage, pay attention to see whether a particular word or phrase seems to hold more than what is on the surface for you. Is there a word or phrase that feels a bit "loaded," as if it might contain an invitation for you within it? Let it simmer in your mind and heart, without feeling the burden of needing to figure out its meaning.

- *Reflect*: Slowly and unhurriedly consider what the intersection point might be between your life and that loaded word or phrase. How and where is your life touched by that word today?

- *Respond*: Slowly and unhurriedly consider what your response to God is. Is God inviting you to do or be something, and what is your honest response?

- *Rest*: As important as anything that may or may not have happened in the process above is that we can return to simply being with God—as we described in the previous chapter as praying without words. So at this point in *lectio divina*, whether or not any particular word or phase has grabbed us, we can trust that grace is working and we can rest with gratitude, perhaps aided by the words from Psalm

116: "Return, O my soul, to your rest, for the LORD has dealt bountifully with you."[55]

Reading with the Mind

I am genuinely no longer that young minister who sat in my office one day and realized I was drawn to prayer but didn't really like the Bible all that much. I have moved much farther toward being the little boy in Rosa's that can't get enough of the honey. I love this stuff. There's plenty of it that I don't understand. I'll never be a Bible scholar. I can't tell you any more than two or three words in Greek or Hebrew and have never taken a class in either one. But the prayer that welled up in me that day in my office years ago—that I would come to sincerely love the Bible—has come to pass and continues to come to pass.

Much of the reason for that shift is, thanks to good guidance I have received along the way, due to learning to read in the different ways we are exploring in this chapter. Reading Scripture with our hearts and reading with our minds are not mutually exclusive—as if we have to choose which approach we think is the right one—although they are very different from one another. Yet if we can hang on to each of them, and learn to have rhythms of both in our lives, we will see a kind of synergy take place in our lives with God as the Scripture is given space to become an ever more wide open channel for God's grace to grow us.

I sometimes entertain myself by compiling a list of Bible verses that, if we were to make plaques out of them, would never sell very well in Christian bookstores. I'll leave it to your imagination to dream about what these plaques might end up looking like, but here are some of my favorites from the list I've occasionally worked on through the years. (Of course there are some doozies that can be found in the Old Testament, but just for the sake of underscoring the point, each of the following either comes from Jesus or Paul.)

- *"When you give a luncheon or a dinner, do not invite...your relatives."*[56]

   (No offense to my beloved family—I'm just quoting the words of our Lord.)

- *"No longer drink only water, but take a little wine for the sake of your stomach and your frequent ailments."*[57]

   (I suppose whether or not this plaque would sell well might depend on the denomination that runs the bookstore. Baptists might consider the plaque condemnable, and Episcopalians might have it on sale right next to the wine rack.)

- *"I tell you, make friends for yourselves by means of dishonest wealth."*[58]

   (This teaching of Jesus has made me scratch my head for years. Surely there's some good explanation about what the original Greek word meant, etc.?)

- *"You cross sea and land to make a single convert, and you make the new convert twice as much a child of hell as yourselves."*[59]

   (I've been a part of a lot of church meetings on the topic of evangelism through the years, but no one has ever brought that verse into the conversation. I long for the day when it happens.)

- *"The weak man eats only vegetables."*[60]

   (I happen to be a member of my state's cattle raisers association. This verse could be our divine mandate.)

———

As the lines above hopefully indicate, we need to interpret the Bible. *Exegesis* is the term for the work of responsibly interpreting a passage of Scripture, and if you and I claim to be followers of an ancient Jewish rabbi, exegesis is inevitably our work to do. Eugene Peterson says, "Without exegesis, spirituality gets sappy, soupy. Spirituality without exegesis becomes self-indulgent....And prayer ends up limping along in sighs and stutters."[61]

Scot McKnight has written a very helpful book along these lines, called *The Blue Parakeet*. He does a masterful job of pointing out ways that we misread the Bible, often based on misunderstandings of what the Bible is. He says that we misread in these ways because of our desire to get something out of the Bible via "shortcuts to grace," while neglecting the thinking and discernment that is necessary to read the Bible well with our minds.[62]

McKnight's chapter on these shortcuts is well worth buying the book. I won't attempt to fully explain all of them here, but here is his list:

• **Morsels of Law**

> *For some, the Bible is a massive collection of laws—what to do and what not to do....God becomes the Law-God, usually a little ticked off and impatient....Yes, commandments aplenty can be found in the Bible. But converting the story of the Bible...into a collection of little more than commandments completely distorts the Bible.*[63]

This is an approach whose extreme example might be that approach of opening the Bible to a random verse thinking that God would always like for you to go out and do whatever it says. If the Bible were a book of laws, we could approach it that way, but that isn't what it is.

• **Morsels of Blessings and Promises**

> *We need to observe what versification did to how we read the Bible. Dividing the Bible up into verses turns the Bible into morsels and leads us to read the Bible as a collection of divine morsels, sanctified morsels of truth.*[64]

In contrast to my imaginary Scripture plaques, these morsels can and do make products that sell well in Christian bookstores. We pause with each morsel to see if we can get something good from it, rather than reading the respective passages from the Bible as a whole. I did a quick search on the website of an online Christian retailer and quickly found numerous such "verse of the day" calendars. One product's description said, "Give the gift of God's word with the Bible Verse-a-Day Mini Calendar. Each page features a pretty floral design on a coordinating background along with the month, date, day of the week, and an encouraging Scripture verse."[65]

In response to the overabundance of Bible-promise-products, McKnight wonders why no one has ever produced a Wrath of God calendar. He goes on: "It's important to know and rely on God's promises....But the blessings and promises of God emerge from a real life's story that also knows that we live in a broken world and some days are tough."[66]

• **Mirrors and Inkblots**

If you show them enough Bible passages and you get them to talk about them, you will hear what is important to them, whether it's in the Bible or not! They'll see their political beliefs, or their thoughts about how to run a church.[67]

McKnight has a great example of how this inkblot shortcut plays out: He gives students a test each semester in one of his classes that asks them to fill out a list of questions on what they think Jesus' personality was like, and then, with the same questions asked in different ways, answer questions about their own personality. The amazing result is that practically everyone thinks Jesus is just like themselves! He says, "Even though we like to think we are becoming more like Jesus, the reverse is probably more the case: we try to make Jesus like ourselves."[68]

• **Puzzling Together the Pieces to Map God's Mind**

[It's as if] God has scattered his mind throughout the Bible, and he gives to us, his readers, the challenge of putting the puzzle together....What's the problem here? Mastery. Those who have solved the puzzle think they've got the Bible mastered....God did not give the Bible so we could master him or it; God gave the

Bible so we could live it, so we could be mastered by it. The moment we think we've mastered it, we have failed to be readers of the Bible. Of course, I think we should read the Bible and know it—but it is the specific element of reading for mastery versus reading to be mastered that grows out of this shortcut.[69]

One of the problems with this approach is that it allows us to always ignore the pieces of the puzzle that don't fit. This is how Christian groups can disagree so vehemently with each other while each considers themselves to be securely on the higher biblical ground while doing so. I find the pieces that fit the puzzle I'm working on while I ignore the other pieces. McKnight quotes Eugene Peterson:

The most frequent way we have of getting rid of the puzzling or unpleasant difficulties in the Bible is to systematize it, organizing it according to some scheme or other that summarizes "what the Bible teaches." If we know what the Bible teaches, we don't have to read it anymore, don't have to enter the story and immerse ourselves in the odd and unflattering and uncongenial way in which the story develops, including so many people and circumstances that have nothing to do, we think, with us.[70]

- **Maestros**

[Many people] *"go to the Bible to find to find the master, the uber-Rabbi—Jesus—at work. Then, when they get up from their reading of the Bible, they imitate the maestro Jesus. 'What would Jesus do?' is the only question they ask. The problem here is the word 'only.'"*[71]

Treating Jesus as master certainly is a good thing for a Christian to do, but what McKnight is getting at in his final shortcut is the tendency to look at the whole of the Bible through one of its authors (or its characters in the case of Jesus). We are then left to either ignore or wonder why the rest of the Bible doesn't put things the way that our maestro does.

I'm guilty of each of these shortcuts, including this one. During all of the years I have been involved with Christian ministries, I have taught and preached discipleship. The invitation to live as a disciple of Jesus is the language of the gospels and of the book of Acts. But then (at least in the way the books are ordered in our Bibles) Paul comes along, and there's no more talk about disciples! How could he do that to me? How could he do that to *Jesus*?

On the other hand, there are a lot of folks whose maestro is Paul, and they can look at Jesus and—surely subconsciously— think, "Why in the world does Jesus never talk about justification by faith?"

McKnight says, "Reading the Bible in the maestro's eyes gives us one chapter in the story of the Bible. One-chapter Bible readers develop one-chapter Christian lives."[72]

And for the sake of trying to set a personal record for quotations included in a chapter, Eugene Peterson says it very well: "It takes the whole Bible to read any part of the Bible."[73]

———

If the task of reading with our minds requires that we get past these shortcuts, how else are we to read? McKnight suggests "In your hand is a Bible that God gave you to read. God asks us to read this Bible as the unfolding of the story of his ways to his people."[74]

In my own attempts to unlearn the shortcuts and replace them with this way of reading the Bible as the unfolding story of God's ways to God's people, I have found N.T. Wright's characterization of that story as a five-act play to be very helpful.[75] Through this lens, we can see each part of the Scripture as fitting into one of these acts of the play:

1. Creation
2. Fall
3. Israel
4. Jesus
5. Church

With that model in mind, I can make sense of some things that prove to be big problems with the Scripture when I read them through the shortcuts. For example, as a young person, I can remember encountering a version of the "maestro" shortcut that said something like, "all you really need is Jesus, so there is no need to spend time reading the Old Testament." When, instead of that, I read the gospels as act four of the play, the Old Testament becomes irreplaceable. (How could I ever hope to have any reliable understanding of act four without paying a lot of attention to acts one through three?)

Another notable quality of Wright's model is that it includes all of Scripture and also leaves act five unfinished. While we can trust from the earlier parts of the play that the closing scene will consist of God making all things new (and, perhaps, beginning a glorious sequel), we can also see that this story is not just about ancient people in ancient places. It is the story in which we are playing a part right now. If I want to live my part of the story well, my task is to read and understand the previous parts that have already been written.

Reading with the Church

When I began to experiment with these ways of reading the Bible, I found a way that freed me from feeling like I needed to pick what to read. I always seemed to end up reading my favorite passages, or to start in Genesis with the thought of making it to Revelation (and, *man*, that bogs down for a long time once you get into Leviticus). At the time, I was on staff at a church where our pastor preached each week from the church's lectionary[76], which is a calendar of four readings for each Sunday of the year (plus other special days, like

Christmas and Holy Week)—one each from the Old Testament, Psalms, epistles, and gospels. I had a devotional book structured around that same calendar[77], so I began to read those four passages repeatedly during the week, and then my pastor would preach from one of them on Sunday.

After making that my normal practice for a number of years, and after learning about the dynamics we have discussed in this chapter, I began to notice ways in which reading according to the lectionary calendar could easily contain some space for a rhythm of both reading with the heart and reading with the mind. Doing so engaged my intellect, as the lectionary would take me to passages I never would have gone to on my own—particularly in the Old Testament. In terms of Wright's analogy, every week, I am repeatedly reading passages from at least three of the acts of the play. During weeks when some extra time presents itself, I will often read some background on one or more of the passages from the notes in my Bible or from a commentary.[78] Since the lectionary rotates in a three-year cycle, over time, my understanding of the full five-act play is growing and deepening through these habits of reading with my mind.

Reading with the lectionary has also given me more space for reading with my heart, in a way that I've come to think of as my "longer lectio." Here is one experience I remember with my longer lectio process from fairly recently.

The psalm for the week was Psalm 19, which is one I have read quite a bit. If I am only in the mode of reading with my mind, I find that I tend to skip familiar passages, or at least skim them, because of a feeling that I already know what they say. Yet it isn't unusual that those familiar passages provide the most fertile soil for reading with the heart. It's as if not being occupied with figuring out what the passage says allows my mind to relax a bit, and—*if* I'll stick with the practice rather than moving on as if there were some hurry—opens some space for the tables to turn so that I can better allow the passage to *read me*. Here's how it happened that particular week.

The final verse of Psalm 19 is the most familiar for many of us:

Let the words of my mouth and the meditation of my heart
be acceptable to you,
O LORD, my rock and my redeemer.

Since it was the most familiar part of the passage, I'm sure that I passed right over it when I first read it on Monday of that week. But when I'm intentional about this longer lectio process, I try to keep reading the four passages for the week—maybe twice a day—until one of them has the feeling of being loaded for me. During that week, I was surprised to have Psalm 19's final verse grab me during one of the re-readings. There was something about the phrases, "words of my mouth" and "meditation of my heart," combined with the prayer that they could be acceptable to God that made me pause—even raising some emotion in me.

I didn't know why the verse felt charged, but I was learning to stick with the lectio divina process, seeking to open myself to the passage rather than take control of it. So I began—as often as I could think of to do so—to pray, "let the words of my mouth and the meditation of my heart be acceptable to you." It might have been ten times in a day, or it might have been fifty. Even if I wasn't in a particularly attentive day, I would at least be reminded of how the verse had grabbed me when I would re-read the verses once each day for the rest of the week.

Then, after a couple of days of letting that verse simmer, praying it as often as I could return my attention to it, I made a connection (or, it is probably more accurate to say that a connection was shown to me). I had been experiencing some significant frustrations in a relationship and I wasn't particularly handling it very well. I had slipped into some bad patterns of stewing over the frustrations, which—of course—

only served to magnify them. My attitude was becoming less and less loving. I certainly wasn't enjoying it, but I didn't know what to do about it.

"Let the words of my mouth and the meditation of my heart be pleasing to you...*Oh. That's it.*" The meditations of my heart regarding that relationship had been selfish and anything but pleasing to God. And they were beginning to make their way into my words to others through complaints, or just by being impatient because my mind was so caught up in the task of ruminating. Now, I didn't have a solution to the problems, but I had a place to start. Each time I noticed my mind going down the familiar selfish-and-frustrated path, it now became a reminder to return to Psalm 19. The next movement of lectio was happening, as I became aware of the point of intersection between my life and the week's passage.

From there, I could continue in the lectio divina process, spending a few minutes later in the week writing in my journal about how I might need to respond since that verse seemed to hold so much for me at that point. After doing so, and for the remainder of the week, I could continue to prayerfully return to the week's readings, both by re-reading the lectionary's passages each day and allowing my mind to go back to Psalm 19's concluding prayer as often as it could.

Both the words of my mouth and the meditation of my heart really needed grace that week, as they also often have since. But I likely would not have opened myself to that grace if it were not for this practice of reading with the Church, of praying Psalm 19 repeatedly, together with millions of other Christians around the world who would also read the same passages that same week. It allowed me to go to that part of the story when Psalm 19 was written, along with the week's other respective passages, and it gave me the chance to not only let the story sink a bit further into me for the week, but also for it to take hold at some deeper levels so that the work of grace could continue in ways that I could not have made happen for myself.

———

Practice

Try your own "longer lectio" this week:

- Visit http://lectionary.library.vanderbilt.edu to see the readings for this week from the Revised Common Lectionary, keeping in mind that millions of Christians around the world will also be reflecting on those same passages this week. (Or a very helpful printed resource with the calendar of readings is *A Guide to Prayer for All Who Walk with God* by Rueben P. Job.[79])

- Read the four passages for the week each day (there is almost always one from the Old Testament, a psalm, an epistle, and a gospel).

- With repeated prayerful readings, it is likely that at least one of the passages will seem to hold something for you. Perhaps it raises an emotion in you, or stirs a longing, or even a dislike. Once that surfaces, hold on to the phrase that grabbed you, without feeling a need to figure it out. Memorize it or carry it around on a card with you, allowing it to "roll around" in your mind as often as possible during the week.

- Don't force a personal meaning for the passage. Rather, stay in that stage of "chewing on it" for the remainder of the week if no particular intersection with your current experience surfaces.

- But if you do become aware of some part of your life that needed to hear that part of the passage, move to the next movement of *lectio divina*, reflecting prayerfully on how God might be inviting you to respond.

- Always feel the invitation to return to rest in God. Even if the verse is one that brings you conviction as Psalm 19 did for me, it will not be shaming. Sometimes, you might not be aware of any of the passages holding any meaning, which is okay. There is no need to force anything from a passage. The point is simply that you are opening yourself to grace through the Scripture, entrusting yourself and whether anything happens to God. Rest again with gratitude, perhaps aided by the words from Psalm 116: "Return, O my soul, to your rest, for the LORD has dealt bountifully with you."

Six

COMMUNION

My flesh is true food and my blood is true drink. Those who eat my flesh and drink my blood abide in me, and I in them.

John 6:55-56

Thirdly. All who desire an increase of the grace of God are to wait for it in partaking of the Lord's Supper.[80]

John Wesley

In drawing aside for lengthy periods of time, we seek to rid ourselves of the corrosion of soul that accrues from constant interaction with others and the world around us. In this place of quiet communion, we discover again that we do have souls, that we indeed have inner beings to be nurtured. Then we begin to experience again the presence of God in the inner sanctuary, speaking to and interacting with us. We understand anew that God will not compete for our attention. We must arrange time for our communion with Him as we draw aside in solitude and silence.[81]

Dallas Willard

IN THE MORE THAN FORTY YEARS since my dad planted his pecan orchard, time has taken its toll. Some trees are big, strong, and have produced a lot of pecans through the years. Other trees have withered and died.

The puzzling thing to me about the different results is that it is not unusual for a withered tree to be adjacent to a strong, old, fruitful tree. They've both been irrigated the same amount. They received the same sunlight, and the exact same care was given to each of them. Yet one of them flourished while the other one dried up. The result is that most of the trees are still there, still growing with one another after all of this time. A significant number of other trees, though, now have their place in stacks of dry firewood.

A look at my life with God would be similar. God's grace has always been available to me in super-abundance, with everything at hand which is needed to live a life fully connected to God and others. At times my life has brought about some good things and I have loved God and people well. At other times, I haven't had much life in me, but have only been dry and useless.

The good news is, that unlike a pecan tree, I have the response-ability to reconnect when I notice some of the warning signs of withering. I can get back into the conditions conducive to my growth, and allow God's good grace to have its effect on me.

I think this is something of the dynamic Jesus was describing when he said in the hours just before his arrest,

Abide in me as I abide in you. Just as the branch cannot bear fruit by itself unless it abides in the vine, neither can you unless you abide in me. I am the vine, you are the branches. Those who abide in me and I in them bear much fruit, because apart from me you can do nothing. Whoever does not abide in me is thrown away like a branch and withers; such branches are gathered, thrown into the fire, and burned. If you abide in me, and my words abide in you, ask for whatever you wish, and it will be done for you. My Father is glorified by this, that you bear much fruit and become my disciples.[82]

Christians throughout the centuries have experienced and then sought to describe this kind of "co-abiding" life with Christ to which Jesus pointed us with this image of the vine and its branches. In this chapter, we will explore that kind of life of abiding in Christ through one big idea (communion) and two ancient practices (the Lord's Supper/Eucharist and solitude).

You and I are these seeds who are learning how to stay planted in the ground over the long haul and allow God's gift of grace to grow us into being fully and truly who we are. In the previous two chapters, we have explored prayer and reading the Scriptures as two indispensable means of God's grace into us throughout this process of God delivering us into our own lives to the full.

Although perhaps you might not have found all of the particular approaches to those practices we explored to be familiar, suggesting that it's a good idea for Christians to pray and read our Bibles probably didn't come as a shock to anyone. I don't expect this book to get any five-star reviews based on the novelty of thinking to include those two practices.

Yet even if their inclusion wasn't unconventional, my hope in writing about them is that we can close the gap between thinking, "I know that's important, and I should do it more [someday]" and how we actually experience them. Then, over time we can experience more of the gift of grace through our practices of prayer and reading the Bible.

If we picture ourselves as a seed in the ground, planted in the orchard, hopefully we can see that if we were to go a month without prayer, we will most likely experience some dryness. Likewise with reading the Scripture—if we go too long without it, we might notice ourselves beginning to wither. I also hope that our metaphor helps us to understand that the withering doesn't come because God is disappointed in us for failing to keep up, but simply because an important channel of receptivity has been closed. [83]

What if you were to imagine yourself going more than a month without receiving the Lord's Supper/the Eucharist? (Just to clarify: I'll use those two terms interchangeably through the remainder of the chapter.) Or what if you were to picture yourself going a month without a significant amount of time alone in solitude with God? Do you envision that the absence of those practices have the same withering effect?

A big part of your response to those questions probably depends on which tradition of Christianity you call home. If your roots are in a tradition that celebrates the Lord's Supper each week, it may be likely that you see it as at least as central a means of grace for you as prayer and Scripture reading. Other Christian traditions which practice it once per quarter, or even not at all, will obviously tend to see it differently. Or, if you are part of a church that emphasizes contemplative practices such as silence during times of worship together, you will be more likely to view solitude as a necessity than Christians from churches where silence in a worship service might only ever occur during a power outage. (And even then, things like generators or megaphones might be on hand to avoid the awkwardness of such a dreadfully quiet moment.)

While recognizing that the practices in this chapter are viewed in very diverse ways by folks in different places along the Christian spectrum, my hope is that after reading about them, you might a) gain an appreciation for how some other Christians view these practices, even if it doesn't match the understanding of your particular branch, and/or b) see the unique places that the Eucharist and solitude might have in developing your openness to a life of abiding in our vine—a life of communion with God.

"Take, eat; this is my body....
Drink from it, all of you; for this is my blood."

In his brief but very helpful book, *The Meal Jesus Gave Us*, N.T. Wright illumined the meaning and practice of the Eucharist for me with the simple comparison to a birthday party.

The birthday party says two things in particular. 'Jane, we wish you a very happy birthday today; and we're glad that, ten years ago, today, you made your grand appearance into the world.' The party joins together the past event and the present moment....It also looks into the future: 'Many happy returns of the day!' we say, even to a ninety-two-year old. Somehow past, present, and future are held together in this one meal.[84]

Wright then continues and applies this past/present/future dynamic of a birthday party to the celebration of the Lord's Supper. I hope that you may already see a connection here to an earlier chapter in which we described biblical salvation in three tenses: I have been saved, I am being saved, and I will be saved. The connection is important, because although we don't often do things like wear party hats or hang streamers, perhaps characterizing the Eucharist as a salvation party could go a long way to helping us become more aware of these three "tenses" of the Lord's Supper.

Communion Past:
"On the night in which he gave himself up for us, he took bread...he took the cup..."[85]

Sometimes we tend to think of the events of Jesus' life, particularly during the week leading up to his crucifixion, as being a script that had been written for him, in which he was the main actor but had no real freedom to change any of the story. I don't think that is true. When we are able to read the gospel stories with some fresh lenses, it becomes easier to see Jesus as being in control of what was happening from beginning to end in his adult life. He intentionally timed his return to Jerusalem, knowing that conflict, arrest, and execution was coming. He used his most confrontational words and actions toward the religious authorities during that week, and for our purposes here, we want to highlight that he chose for all of the events of Holy Week to take place *at Passover*. He did so in order to explain the events of the week to his disciples—by the words and actions they would share together during their Passover meal.

Luke mentions that Jesus said he had been eagerly waiting to share that Passover meal with his disciples before he suffered. They ate together and they went through the rituals that every one of them had participated in every year of their lives at Passover. The traditions went back to the time of Moses, somewhere around 1,200-1,500 years prior to that meal between Jesus and his disciples. They ate the meal in certain ways, doing the right things and saying the right words at the right times, in order to re-tell (and really to re-*live*) the story of their ancestors' exodus from Egypt, how God delivered them from their slavery and sent them on to the promised land. Every part of the meal was orchestrated in order to re-tell and re-live that central salvation story.

Jesus' disciples would have been very aware of the past-present-future dynamic of the meal. As they sought to relive the story of their ancestors' deliverance it was a very tangible realization of who they were in the present, because of what God had done to rescue them in the past. They participated in the ritual each year as a way of ingraining their identity, as if to say, "this is who we are, because this is who we were."

Elements of the meal also clearly pointed them toward their future. The meal in the upper room that night was a salvation party, and everyone sharing it with Jesus was daily aware of their people's desperation to be delivered from oppressors all over again. They faithfully believed God would again act to save them and all of the old promises from their prophets could finally and fully be fulfilled. The meaning of what they did each year in those Passover meals had always been held together by what God had done in their past, and what they trusted that God would do in their future, as if to say, "this is who we are, and this is where we are headed, because this is who we were."

It's important for us to realize that for Jews of any time, celebrating this Passover feast is not just *recalling* an event from their nation's past, like citizens of the United States might do with Presidents' Day or even Independence Day. Rather, it was a way of *participating* in the story from the past that shaped their present identity and their future hope. It was their way of counting themselves among those whom God delivered from slavery in Egypt as well as those whom they hoped God would deliver from the brutal oppression of Rome. As Steve Harper notes, "Truly to remember something or someone meant more than recollection. It meant to recall an event so thoroughly that the event comes alive, anew and afresh in the present."[86]

Think for a moment of the implications for us of that kind of remembering in regard to Jesus' statement during this meal, "Do this in remembrance of me." In the sense of memory that was central to everyone's participation that night with Jesus in Jerusalem, it is a recognition that we are not observers in the story, but that we are invited to be participants. We are invited to join in the salvation party which took place on the evening before Jesus' arrest.

We can picture Jesus there as the rabbi, saying the words which the head of the family would say during the meal. The disciples all would have known the routine by memory. Each of their fathers had said those words year after year. Jesus and the disciples were making their way through the story when at some point in the meal, Jesus deviated from the script. Instead of saying words to link the bread and the wine back to the Exodus and forward to the final liberation of Israel, he said new words, which linked them powerfully to *himself* and the death he very shortly would die.

Sitting at a secret meal in Jerusalem, Jesus was saying, by what he was doing as much as by the words he was speaking: "This is the moment. This is the time. And it's all because of what's going to happen to me." Jesus gathered more than a thousand years of Jewish Passover history before him and put new meaning into it, signifying that he was about to do what Moses had done, to lead God's people into freedom. But when he broke that bread and passed that cup, he indicated that he would do so by taking everything upon himself, by letting himself be the sacrifice and letting his own blood seal the covenant.

"Do this in remembrance of me." The next time you are with your church and you hear those words, recognize, "this is who we are, because this is who we were"—a group of clumsy disciples gathered for a salvation party around a meal with our rabbi, who unforgettably took all the oppression of the past onto himself and so generously invited us to eat, drink, and abide in him.

Communion Present:
"Pour out your Holy Spirit on us gathered here, and on these gifts of bread and wine. Make them be for us the body and blood of Christ, that we may be for the world the body of Christ, redeemed by his blood."[87]

My wife and I were missionaries in Guatemala for two years. We went there to work with a children's home, but for our first several months we were in another city learning Spanish. People often say that immersion is the way to go when trying to learn a language, and they're right, but they leave out how intense that immersion feels when you are going through it. These Spanish classes were not like what I experienced in high school. Instead, we—who spoke no Spanish—each had daily four-hour one-on-one classes with teachers who spoke no English, and we had to figure out how to make some progress.

In addition, during that time we also lived with a Guatemalan family who spoke no English. As you can imagine, those early dinner conversations were pretty limited.

The weekends gave us a break from the intensity of our classes, but not from that of the immersion. We found a Guatemalan church to attend on Sunday mornings. Being 6'7" in a country where there aren't many people who are even 5'7", it was obvious in church (and everywhere) that I was a long, long way from fitting in. Yet the church's services had enough familiarity in them that we could have a clue what was going on even in those early days when we could understand *muy poquito* of the language. Sometimes the folks in the church would sing a song to which we would recognize the tune, and their services flowed generally like we were used to, so although we felt really out of place, we weren't completely lost.

The church there served the Lord's Supper once a month, and our early days there helped me to appreciate some things about Communion that had never really sunk in before.

Even though we didn't understand the words to the songs, nor the words in the prayers, nor the words in the sermon, nor the words people said when speaking directly to us, I quickly came to eagerly look forward to the Sundays when the Eucharist would be served, because it was the only time that I felt like I could really participate. It was the thing in our worship that we could count on to faithfully *communicate* to us, even though the language barrier felt so difficult to us in the beginning.

It was a wonderful thing to be able to come right alongside these people, who were from seemingly an entirely different world than we were, to receive Jesus' body and blood together. In that moment, the language barrier was overcome, and it didn't matter if we were the only gringos in the whole place, because it was about the body and blood of Christ offered generously and equally to everyone. It was our chance for all of us, together, to invite the Lord to dwell in the deepest parts of us, and there was certainly a sense in which we were doing so not only across the cultural and language barriers, but together with two thousand years of other followers of Jesus— from every time and place in the world.

A while later, once we began to understand and speak the language quite a bit better, we discovered an unexpected downside of becoming bilingual: when you don't understand what the pastor is saying, for all you know, it may be the best sermon you've ever heard. Once you can understand it, you become aware of how the sermon can fall flat in any language.

Even that, though, increased my longing for those Sundays when we would share the Eucharist, because there was a real sense in which I knew that the service would be much less dependent on what the pastor said, and there would come a moment when the message of Christ would be communicated in its fullness every time—when we were invited to receive Jesus' body broken for us, and his blood shed for us.

Whether or not you have experienced a time when you noticed yourself looking forward to a chance to receive the Lord's Supper, even longing for it, I hope that this at least helps us to set the stage for looking at some important questions about it: What is it that we are doing when we do this together? What is it that takes place, then and there in that moment, that makes it different from other moments?

———

The New Testament insists that this is to be one of the most powerful signs of our unity as followers of Jesus. Yet Christian history has played out in a way that, rather than always reminding us of our unity in Christ, disagreements over the Eucharist have been some of the most serious and costly divisions between different groups in the overall church. So while recognizing that different groups of Christians see these things in different ways, my aim is to explore the core of the practice, which—if we can live into it—could deepen any Christian's experience of receiving the Lord's Supper.

Perhaps one important part of learning to deepen your appreciation for your own church's practice of the Lord's Supper while also increasing your respect for that of other groups is to realize that there are ways in which the Eucharist today is something different for all of us than it was for the earliest generations of Christians. In the very early days of the

Church, this was still an actual full meal which groups of disciples would share together in someone's home. It gets mentioned in Paul's letters in the ways that it does because it had become a deeply ingrained practice for Christians in those first decades after Jesus' Passover meal with his disciples in Jerusalem. From those letters we learn that the very early church would share their meal together, and there would come a point when they would tell the story of Jesus' last night with his disciples. They were careful to tell the story with particular words when it came to talking about bread being broken and wine being poured, in order to make the connection to the night in that upstairs room, as part of a full meal.

Then, as time progressed, the custom changed to being closer to what we do today, which we might call a "token meal." Yes, we are getting a small amount of food and drink, but the bodily nourishment that comes to us through it isn't at all part of the intention as it would be with a full meal. So over time, different groups asked different kinds of questions about what it is that happens when we do this together, and have come to different conclusions about it.

Without going further into the history and debates about it, I'll try to summarize like this: virtually all Christians who practice the Lord's Supper agree that in some real way, Christ is present with them when they gather together for this practice. Many of the debates have focused on different understandings of *how* Christ is present (Do the bread and wine change in some way, or not? Are they just symbols, or is there more to them?) Representing an effort to find the common ground, I appreciate the note in my Bible—of which our past/present/future framework is an echo—which says, "Our greater concern is about time rather than space: it is more important to say *why* Christ is present *now* than to explain *how* one might say that Christ is present *here*."[88]

On one level, I can say with some confidence there will be agreement among Christians regarding Jesus' presence when we receive the Eucharist, because there is widespread agreement among Christians that Christ is *always* present with us. Therefore, I'm not exactly going out on a limb with the statements made to this point. But I do want to push it a little further and say that yes, Christ is always with us, and this past/present/future framework gives us a way of understanding how a quality of Jesus' presence is different when we gather together as his people and do as he instructed us with bread and wine.

As we explored in the previous section, we believe that when we "do this in remembrance" of Jesus in the present, there is a real sense in which we are there with the disciples at their last supper together, as well as together with all of the followers of Jesus throughout the centuries who have done this in remembrance of him. This is who we are, because of that meal in the past with all that it meant and all who have shared in it from then until now. It is as if the past comes up into the present moment and gives its foundation, context and meaning. And, as we'll explore in the next section, we also believe that the future comes bursting into the present as the Lord's Supper is a real foretaste of what is to come when God makes everything new, and as Jesus said, we will eat the Passover again with him when it finds its fulfillment in the kingdom of God.[89]

The past and the future, both focused on this meal in Jesus' presence, both come rushing together into *this* moment that we call "right now," putting us in Jesus' presence in the present in a way that is different from how we are with God throughout the rest of our lives. Understanding this practice as a means of grace helps us to see the place that it can play in giving more space for Christ to abide in us, and us in him, so that all of our lives can be more grace-full and enabled to become channels of that grace to the world around us.

Communion Future:
"By your Spirit make us one with Christ, one with each other, and one in ministry to all the world, until Christ comes in final victory and we feast at his heavenly banquet."[90]

After my dad died, I remember being at the funeral home for the visitation from family and friends. It's common in those situations for people to make well-intentioned comments as they attempt to comfort the grieving. Often, the simplest comments communicate that the most effectively. For example, I remember my high school's football coach coming into the visitation, getting a little choked up, and saying about my dad in regard to his quiet and gentle manner, "You always felt like you were somebody just because he knew your name."

On the other hand, we often feel like we need to fix the problem for the grieving person, so we try to alleviate their pain with a spiritual assurance. Any time you are in grief, a number of these kinds of comments are sure to come your way, and they often reveal some very popular yet unscriptural notions about what awaits us after we die. One particular comment took the prize after my dad died and provided some theological comic relief. I wasn't offended by it, but laughed quite a bit about it afterward, because it reflects some of these ideas about heaven that so many sincere people have.

I was standing there greeting people as they came in the door. A woman came in whom I didn't know, and I'm sure she introduced herself and mentioned the connection to someone in the family, but I don't remember it. Then she asked me something, and at first, I thought it was a pretty good question. She said, "Do you think that we have to learn how to do things in heaven?"

I wasn't sure what she meant, but I said, "Sure, I guess there's something of a learning curve there."

Then she said, "Yeah, I think so too. Like learning to fly. So maybe whenever it gets hard for your mom, it might help her just to picture your dad up there learning to fly with his new wings."

I have no idea how I responded to her. I have no reason to doubt her sincerity, but her comment reflected ideas that are more influenced by *Precious Moments* figurines than they are by the Hebrew and Christian Scriptures. The time-enduring hope of Christians through the ages is *not* that we will sprout wings, bounce around in the clouds, play harps, and endure some kind of interminable church service. Instead, our hope is that what happened to Jesus at his resurrection will one day happen to us all—and indeed to all of creation, as heaven and earth are finally and fully joined together forever. Jesus will be reigning as king, and you and I will be there, living *human* lives, carrying on his work.

Dallas Willard says, "We will not sit around looking at one another or at God for eternity but will join the eternal Logos, 'reign *with* him,' in the endlessly ongoing creative work of God. It is for this that we were each individually intended."[91] Willard and N.T. Wright have both written masterfully about this, helping to re-biblicize our ideas about the future. Wright says:

> Some people think of the Christian's "promised land" as simply "heaven." Some even think that this could be rather boring. How wrong they are. In Paul's writings, the Christian's "promised land" is the entire renewed world. If we die before the time, we will go to "heaven", that is, into God's dimension of existence. But the long-term hope is that all those in "heaven" and presently on earth will be transformed, re-embodied, to join in the new life when...God will make new heavens and a new earth. Within this transformation of reality, Jesus himself will be personally present. Every longing of our hearts will be satisfied in our meeting with him and being nourished by his presence and his love.[92]

To my memory, Jesus only specifically mentioned one thing that he would do with us, after what has already happened to him in his resurrection happens also to all of us and to all of creation—after everything is made new: "But I tell you, from this moment I will not drink of this fruit of the vine until that day when I drink it in a new way in my Father's kingdom with you."[93]

> *Every time that we do this in the present from now until then, it is an advance participation in what, one day, we will do again with him.*

In other words, we will again enjoy the "this" that we now do in remembrance of him when we share it *with* him, when all things are made new. Every time that we do this in the present from now until then, it is an advance participation in what, one day, we will do again with him.

———

Since I'm someone who enjoys books and history, a number of years ago, my wife surprised me with the gift of being able to attend a book signing by a former U.S. president. I gladly stood in a long, winding line for hours. As I did so, famous scenes from his presidency replayed in my mind. This man I had read about, and had seen on television so often, played a central role in moments that left indelible marks on history and on my memory.

After hours of waiting in the line that wound through different rooms, I finally passed some secret service agents, turned a corner and could see him. This person about whom I knew so many stories was suddenly right there in plain sight. A couple of minutes later, I was standing in front of him, and we were exchanging greetings and looking one another in the eye.

1 John states emphatically, "What we do know is this: when he is revealed, we will be like him, for *we will see him* as he is"[94]—not a former politician or celebrity, but the one around

whom history has been shaped more than any other; the one about whom more pages have been written and more songs sung than anyone else; the one whom you sensed drawing you closer at some point in your life and is with you even as you have been reading these words; the one whose grace is growing you; who said, "abide in me, and I will abide in you," and "do this in remembrance of me." *He* will be in our sight, in *resurrected human flesh*, and you and I will share a meal with him even as we then—finally—fully draw our lives from him.

Jesus repeatedly told stories about banquets. He changed water into wine at a wedding meal. He shared this Passover feast with his disciples on his last night with them.

In the traditional Eucharist liturgy, we repeat and insist that "Christ has died. Christ is risen. Christ will come again," and I love the line that says we do this "until Christ comes in final victory and we feast together at his heavenly banquet."

Right before John's vision of everything being made new in the last two chapters of Revelation, he is told, "Blessed are those who are invited to the wedding supper of the lamb."[95]

Then in those last two chapters of Revelation, we have the vision of the union of heaven and earth being consummated, and the celebration being a wedding feast. That feast will undoubtedly have a lot to do with the Passover, yet will also be new, and we will in some mysterious way both feast *with* and *on* the one who said "this is my body...this is my blood."

This is who we are, because this is who we were, and this is where we are headed.

"The apostles gathered around Jesus, and told him all that they had done and taught. He said to them, 'Come away to a deserted place all by yourselves and rest a while.'"

As a college student, I was once in charge of finding a few people to help our campus pastor serve the Lord's Supper in one of our chapel services. I knew that one of my basketball teammates had a deep faith which I admired, so I asked him to help. He kindly said that he would do so, and then added, "but I'm a Quaker. We don't take the Lord's Supper. But I'll still help you serve."

At that moment, I remembered my initial surprise at earlier finding out about his Quaker roots, since I had never seen him wear a big hat nor eat oatmeal. By my unintended actions, I kept making it painfully clear to him that I knew absolutely nothing about the Quaker church—including that they don't wear the hats of the guy on the oatmeal box, nor necessarily eat his products—plus, as I found out that day, they do not practice the Eucharist.

I had enough respect for my friend that I didn't question his non-practice of the Lord's Supper, but for years I chalked it up as something of a quirk of his tradition. Years later, however, as my own desperation for a more grace-full way of life with God drove me to experiment with some more "radical" means of grace like solitude and silence, I began to read and learn a lot from various Quaker authors. While I had been dabbling in these practices that felt somewhat extreme in my circles, it was significant for me to realize how my friend's tradition had been making them central throughout their history.

One paragraph in particular took me back to that day as a college student, when I asked my Quaker friend to help me and he humbly did so even though it was outside of his custom. In a book exploring the centrality of silence in Quaker worship and spirituality, J. Brent Bill says,

> *The only thing I can compare it to is the [Roman] Catholic belief that in the "celebration of Mass...Christ is really present through Holy Communion to the assembly gathered in His name." It is the same way with silence for Quakers....We believe that when our hearts, minds, and souls are still, and we wait expectantly in holy silence, that the presence of Christ comes among us."[96]*

It clicked for me. It wasn't that my friend did not want communion. It was that, while I had been exploring communion with God through the riches of opening the depths of myself to Christ through the Lord's Supper, his tradition was teaching him to seek communion with God through solitude and silence.

Since we have already considered some aspects of the practice of silence in our section on praying without words, we will close this chapter on communion by exploring its companion practice: solitude.

———

My son has a toy train track which we have enjoyed for several years. Ever since my wife and I became parents, we have discovered that it is something of a rarity to find toys that the kids enjoy playing with for years which are also durable enough to last as long as the kids want to play with them. We would, however, give his train track an A+ rating, and it has been well-used.

One day, during the same period of time when I had been desperate enough for more of a grace-conducive way of life to begin experimenting with these practices, my son and I were playing with his trains and I noticed something. Most of the pieces of the toy track are built in a way that, as long as the train is going straight and not too fast around a curve or down a hill, everything will keep going okay and the train won't tip over or crash. But there are a few parts of the track—such as the station—where the rails are essentially inverted, with grooves going into the ground rather than rails coming up out of it. When one of the train cars has gotten a wheel off of the track or is close to falling over and crashing, if the engine can just make it to the station, the whole train will be reset and able to continue.

When I spend a day alone with God, it is like the inverted pieces of the train track. I often come wobbling into those days, closer to tipping and crashing than I may realize. Then the day of solitude inverts the rest of my life—I have no roles to fill for people, no one to impress, and nothing to achieve. All of the things that add up over time and tend to get me moving too fast and headed off-track are gone, and it's as if I go into the ground rather than continuing to barrel along on the surface.

I'll be honest with you, it usually isn't very exciting. I don't come back with great stories to tell. I will inevitably feel some mixture of relief and boredom. But the more I practice it over time, the more I become aware that God is with me in my normal days—and the more I become able to accept the reality of God's love for me and for everyone I encounter.

Henri Nouwen writes:

Solitude is being with God and God alone. Is there any space for that in your life?...It's important because it's the place in which you can listen to the voice of the One who calls you the beloved...to let that voice speak to the center of your being, to your guts, and let that voice resound in your whole being.[97]

In another place, Nouwen says, "the measure of [our] solitude is the measure of [our] capacity for communion."[98]

Having rhythms of these longer times alone with God as part of my lifestyle has become the most central practice I have for staying planted and allowing grace to continue to grow me. While the other various practices we have explored in these three chapters are all time-tested ways of putting more logs on the fire of our life with God through the course of our normal days and weeks, solitude is the practice of putting *me* into that fire. Without solitude, I get too caught up in my own agendas for myself, my family, and the entire world. Without solitude, I mistakenly assume that the things which fluster me are also flustering God. Without solitude, I may remain enrolled in a group that seeks to serve God, but I have very insufficient resources to draw from for the sake of discerning what God might be leading these groups to do and what my role in them should be. And ultimately, without solitude, I find myself less able to love those around me well, because I am less aware of the fondness God has for me—and therefore my default is to defend myself from others rather than naturally becoming an agent of God's grace to them.[99]

———

Practice
- *The Lord's Supper*: Find out when the next time will be that your church will celebrate the Eucharist, and make plans to be there to receive it—regardless of whether it is tomorrow, or next month. Be mindful of your participation in the ancient stories of the Exodus and the Last Supper, of Christ's real presence with you and your church family, and of the foretaste of the day when all of God's people will feast together with Jesus in plain sight.
- *Solitude*: Find someone whom you trust and whose life with God seems to have been forged in their own experiences in solitude and let them know of your desire to have some time alone with God. If they are near your location, they may be able to suggest a place to go. Then, find a time within the next month to spend four to eight hours alone with God. The only real guideline is to be careful to not fill it with much distraction. "What would God and I like to do together during this time?" might be a helpful and freeing question.[100] Sometime after your solitude, have a conversation with the person you found about your experience. Keep in mind thatthe point is how they shape us over time much more so than whether or not we felt like we had a great time while doing them.
- *Communion*: If possible, seek to combine the two practices by having some solitude within the few days before your church next celebrates the Lord's Supper. Then, having emerged from time alone with God, pay attention to whether you receive Christ's body and blood—and the presence of your Christian family receiving them alongside you—any differently.

Part Three

GIVING
GRACE

Seven

GRACE TO YOU AND ME

You have died, and your life is hidden with Christ in God. When Christ who is your life is revealed, then you also will be revealed with him in glory.

Colossians 3:3-4

Christ is ready. And he is all you want. He is waiting for you. He is at the door! Let your inmost soul cry out,

"Come in, come in, thou heavenly Guest!
Nor hence again remove:
But sup with me, and let the feast
Be everlasting love."[101]

John Wesley

We can become like Christ in character and in power and thus realize our highest ideals of well-being and well-doing. That is the heart of the New Testament message.[102]

Dallas Willard

NOT ALL PECANS BECOME TREES. If a seed remains a seed rather than becoming a tree, there could be numerous reasons why that happened. Maybe it was eaten by an animal, preserved in a jar, or baked into a pie. Whatever the cause, a seed that did not become a tree was kept away from the conditions conducive to its growth. Instead, if the conditions for growth are put into place and kept in place, the tree that is hidden in the seed will someday be seen.

Inside of this life that I am living (with all of its activities, all its distractions, all its blessings—everything about it) there is a me that is, in a sense, much bigger than the me I now am. I can do things to prevent that truer and fuller me from ever showing up in the world. I can allow myself to be consumed by any of the endless things in our culture that are constantly clamoring for my attention. (For example, I recently saw an advertisement on a television station saying, "Take our seven day challenge"—and the seven day challenge was to watch their TV station for seven days. I could do that, but it probably is not the best of the options available to me if I want to be truly and fully who I am in Christ.) There are any number of things I could do to take myself out of the grace-conditions in which growth can naturally take place. Doing so will prevent my real life—which is hidden with Christ in God—from ever being seen.

We have talked about grace being life-giving, and we've also talked about how it doesn't always feel that way. Grace takes the old you, and actually kills off some parts of the you which isn't so real and true so that the "you-ier"[103] you that is hidden with Christ in God can grow, flourish, and become fully what it was created to be.

Even once we are convinced that a life of staying planted is the kind we really want, and we genuinely trust God enough to keep ourselves planted and let grace do its good, slow work, a significant obstacle still remains: "Isn't it too late for me? Perhaps God's grace may still be able to grow me into something good, but haven't I already messed up or missed out on too much of the process to talk about becoming *fully* who God created me to be?"[104]

———

When my son was two and my daughter was about to be born, my wife and I looked to the future and wanted our kids to have a good place to play in our yard at home, so we bought a new backyard play set for our kids. It was one of those wooden sets that has swings plus a ladder that goes up to a small clubhouse, and a slide that comes down. And nineteen million tiny pieces of hardware.

The first thing I learned in the process of putting the set together was that I have always drastically underestimated how much work those things take to assemble. When I've seen them in stores, they have looked nice, but somehow my eyes never noticed the immense quantity of screws, bolts, nuts, washers, etc., which they require. I knew I was in trouble when I opened the box and the directions said that even with two or three people, it would still take twelve to fourteen hours to complete. I knew my trouble was doubled when I realized the only person I had to help me was the same two-year-old for whom we bought the set, and any minutes he logged on the job would be more likely to increase the time remaining until the project's completion than it would be to help me finish.

The second thing I learned in the process had to do with all of the mistakes I made in putting it together. There were close to a dozen times that I had pieces put together only to realize that I had made a mistake, and then had to take pieces apart and put them together again. A couple of times there had already been too much progress made before I realized my error, so I had to improvise by putting some piece where it would be good enough, rather than where it was really supposed to go—or by drilling my own holes where the holes would have been if I had done things correctly.

In my younger days, I would have become pretty frustrated at those mistakes, but at this point in my life I've made enough of them to realize that the mistakes are part of the process of getting things right. For example, I have a lot of ideas that have never gotten off of the ground because of the hesitancy brought on by the possibility of the mistakes that I would surely make along the way. And, the projects that have gotten off the ground have, as expected, been full of mistakes.

Which one of those types of projects ends up fulfilling its intended purpose? Obviously, it's the type in which something happens, mistakes included. This is because, *even with the mistakes that have taken place, things can still end up perfectly serving their purpose.*

The play set will permanently show the scars of the errors I made in its assembly. It has some extra holes from my drill, and some hardware doesn't match since I had to go out and get new pieces to make up for my mess-ups. In the end, however, the play set's purpose is that my kids and their friends would enjoy playing on it. Even with its misplaced holes and hardware (a.k.a. its imperfections), it could still perfectly be that which it was made to be.

This helps me to make sense out of a God who knows our mistakes so well and who also says, "Be perfect as your Father in heaven is perfect."[105] What a relief to know that the perfection to which the gospel urges us is something other than a track record completely free of mistakes. I've made plenty of errors in working with God in the process of my own "renovation," but my sincere hope is that there's still a very real way in which I can end up fully accomplishing my purpose— even hoping that my mistakes are part of the process of becoming truly and fully who I am in Christ, someone who consistently acts according to love of God and love of people.

If the people who knew me best can honestly look back at the years of my life and say that I loved God and I loved people—that I had a living, vital relationship with God and passed it on to others— then, because of the immense amount of God's grace in my life, I will have been who I was made to be.

That play set had a life of five years before my tall children outgrew it and we got a bigger one this past year. It was well-used, stayed standing, and never caused any child's serious injury. As a play set in our back yard, its entire existence was a complete success.

Fifty years from now, if the people who knew me best can honestly look back at the years of my life and say that I loved God and I loved people—that I had a living, vital relationship with God and passed it on to others—then, because of the immense amount of God's grace in my life, I will have been who I was made to be.

———

Gordon T. Smith is a theologian whose writings I've recently, quickly, come to value highly. In one of his books, he takes on the task of describing what a mature Christian life looks like. Being the unique creations of an endlessly creative Creator that we are, maturity and fullness of purpose are going to look different for each of us, yet there will also be some common threads, which Smith describes as four invitations.[106]

First, the invitation to each of us to become truly and fully who we are in Christ is an *invitation to become holy through developing wisdom*. That may seem surprising, depending on how you think about what it means to be holy. If holy people are those who excel at following the rules and doing the largest quantity of spiritual stuff, then holiness and wisdom may not go together very well. A person may do all the right stuff (possibly even too much of the right stuff, as with my prayer book on Christmas morning) and not be the kind of person you would go to if you were seeking wisdom.

Throughout this entire book, we are exploring a completely different kind of holiness than that kind of pseudo-sanctity. Since our characterization of a life of devotion to God in this book is one of full cooperation with grace rather than strict avoidance of sin, holiness then becomes utter grace-dependence rather than preoccupation with the degree of our tainted-ness. I become holy as I cooperate with grace and allow it to grow me into being truly and fully who I am in

Christ. In that light, Smith's point that holy people are wise people makes perfect sense. Think of how there is a sense in which it seems tragic to meet older people who are not wise—as Smith says, "to grow older and not wiser is to live poorly, to fail to achieve the purpose for which one lives."[107]

On the other hand, think of an elderly person you have known who sought and developed wisdom through most of their lifetime. When we meet someone like that who has lived a long time, there is a sense—regardless of their circumstances—in which things with them are as they should be.

The next invitation Smith points out is *the invitation to do good work* in response to the call of Christ. That may or may not mean what you do for your job. This is good work in the sense of discovering who God has created you to be—a natural effect of letting yourself be that seed that stays planted in the conditions for its growth. Then the you that is there, hidden with Christ, grows and grows eventually, naturally—and even in a sense *easily*—the tree produces fruit, because that is simply what trees do. Think of doing good work not necessarily as what you do that earns a paycheck, but as what you give yourself to that will last, or your efforts that create things of real value. So, for example, in the stage of life my wife and I are in with young children, a huge part of our work is raising kids (though that undoubtedly takes a lot more money out of our bank account than it puts in). My work also includes managing the family business, accompanying others in spiritual direction, and writing projects like this one—in other words, the kinds of things that are more often considered "work."

Therefore, if we are to truly and fully become who we are in Christ, a significant part of that process will be knowing God and knowing ourselves well enough to be able to make wise decisions about what we give ourselves to and what we do not. Smith points this out in regard to Jesus, saying that not only are we struck and inspired by Jesus' teaching and insights, but also by "the simplicity and focus of his work. He knew his calling; rarely if ever was he rushed or anxious about his ministry. He knew what he had to do and was prepared, quite literally, to die for what mattered. In the end, he was able to say those remarkable words: 'I glorified you on earth by finishing the work that you gave me to do.'"[108]

> *Busyness can be very effective at distracting us from the things conducive to our growth. Busyness can put up all kinds of barriers to grace in our lives and keep that seed from ever germinating.*

He also points out that we need to be careful of our tendency to assume that more is better. Just as it isn't true that the more rules you follow, the holier you are, neither does your holiness increase in direct correlation with your busyness. In fact, as we have all probably experienced, busyness can be very effective at distracting us from the things conducive to our growth. Busyness can put up all kinds of barriers to grace in our lives and keep that seed from ever germinating.

We pay attention to this so that we can, as Smith says, "embrace what we are called to do and graciously [decline] that to which we are not called. We learn to say 'yes' and we learn to say 'no.' Actually, we will likely say 'no' more often than we say 'yes.' And, when we say 'no' it is specifically and precisely so that we can say 'yes' to that to which we are being called."[109]

That idea leads into what is the most important of these four invitations: *the invitation to learn to love.*

I remember a conversation with a friend who had been very successful in a business career and was at a point of looking for something meaningful to give himself to for the rest of his years. The best I could do was to encourage him to essentially carve out the space in his life to let the seed germinate, grow in who he is in Christ, and as he does so—

over time—the fruit that God wants to come from his life will come in a very natural way. In the meantime, he will not be lacking for things to occupy himself in his life with God— because today, and every day for the rest of his life, there are people to love. He has family. He has coworkers. He interacts with people in the grocery store. He goes to church. The central task in becoming who you and I are in Christ is to learn to love. Any discussion of the effects of grace on our lives and of what maturity looks like for a Christian must center on love, or it is something other than the way of Jesus.

And then, the last of Smith's ways of describing the characteristics of a mature life in Christ is to say that we are all *invited to know the joy of God*. Thanks be to God that there is joy, real joy to be found in our lives in Christ! As was the case in the description of wisdom, "joyful" may not be the way we would describe some of the people that come into our minds with the word *holy*. If that is the case, however, our conception of holiness needs some reworking. Just as there's no such thing as a witless holiness, neither is there such a thing as a miserable, crotchety, crabby holiness.

Think of Jesus' last night with his disciples. In the same conversation in which he gives them the invitation "abide in me, and I will abide in you," and he talks about coming with his Father to make their home in them, Jesus also repeatedly talks about his joy being in the disciples. He says, "I'm telling you these things so that my joy may be in you and your joy may be complete."[110]

How do you think they reacted when they heard those words? If Jesus had not exuded joy throughout his life, would they have hung on to his invitation? Would they have said, "ugh—*his* joy? I'll take some of his ability to turn water into wine, but his *joy*? No thanks." No, they had seen his deep, pervasive joy throughout their time with him, and his offer to convey it to them was good, generous news.[111]

Dallas Willard taught about the importance of reflecting on what we imagine the life of God is like. He said that we often think of God as "the great unblinking cosmic stare."[112] Can you leave yourself planted for a lifetime if that Stare is the one who said, "I will be with you always—even to the end of the age"? On the other hand, how do you react to the statement that God is the most joyous being to have ever lived? Willard says, "All of the good and beautiful things from which we occasionally drink tiny droplets of soul-exhilarating joy, God continuously experiences in all their breadth and depth and richness."[113] If we do not believe God to be joyous, then our conceptions of what growing in Christ will be like will inherently be devoid of joy, and we won't be able to give ourselves fully over to the process.

False versions of holiness are presented to us as a life that is burdensome, full of impossible standards to reach, and utterly, always serious. But Jesus—whom the party people loved to be around—said that his joy would be in us, and our joy would be complete.

I love the way James Bryan Smith says it: "The true sign of sanctity is not seriousness, but joy."[114]

We know real, genuine joy when we experience it and when we see it in others. It isn't something we conjure up. It isn't a smile that we force. But it wells up from somewhere in the core of us, and it is all-pervasive because of coming to know—through the days, months, years, and decades of our lives with God—how utterly well-off we are in Christ.

———

What is true in that sense of joy is true of each of these characteristics. Even though they are invitations, in a somewhat counter-intuitive way, they are not things that will surface in our lives by straining after them. We can't get out our *Seven Habits of Highly Effective People* notebook and make an action plan for this year for how we will obtain more wisdom, good work, love, and joy in our lives.

Grace grows these qualities more indirectly than that. They are the good fruit, of the good tree, of the good seed, that has stayed in its conditions for growth over a long period of time. The seed, soil, light, water—even the life and growth themselves—are gifts of a good Creator. These qualities surface in us through the indirect processes of grace, because that grace comes from a Creator from whom we inherit these qualities—because God is wise, does good work, loves, and has and gives joy.

Those characteristics are true of God, and they are true of me when I am fully and truly who I am in Christ. Therefore, if I can allow grace to take its effect on me and grow me into this kind of life, *I will reflect my Creator.* When you see a great tree, or a field of bluebonnets in the Texas hill country, or even when you wear a shirt that feels just right, or play an old guitar that has a great sound[115]—these are good creations which reflect really good creators. *God's creations give God glory by being fully what they are.*

This is more true of us than of those other things, because not only do we reflect our Creator, but in more theological language, when I live this way, *I bear my Creator's image in the world.* As I become truly and fully who I am in Christ—and over time, wisdom, good work, love, and joy naturally emerge from the life of Christ in me—this life that is uniquely mine to live in this world is somehow also God's life. As the wise, working, loving, joyful God cultivates me, pours Christ's own life into me, and I find my life in him just by being what I really am, I experience more and more of what Jesus meant when he said, "abide in me, and I will abide in you."

———

I think this points us toward correcting something that can be a powerful misconception for us. For years, I have thought and taught—and indeed I still believe—that the goal of our lives is to be like Jesus. However, I've come to think about that differently than I used to.

There are ways in which it is very helpful and completely appropriate for us to have being like Jesus as our goal. Primary among them is that Jesus shows us how to allow ourselves to be planted in those conditions for growth. In a sense, taking on his lifestyle is the way that we learn to cooperate with grace. We learn to pray, because Jesus prayed. We spend time in solitude, because Jesus spent time in solitude. We serve others, because Jesus served others. We also certainly learn from his teaching, and being his disciple means very little if it doesn't mean some practical imitation of him.

Yet there are also ways in which being like Jesus makes very little sense for my life. Jesus was a Jewish rabbi in ancient Israel, and his life was his to live. My life in west Texas in the 20th and 21st centuries since his time is very different. His life was his to live, yours is yours to live, mine is mine, and they are all different. So strapping on some sandals and going out and trying to recruit some fishermen to follow me probably isn't the kind of life for which God has me in this world. Having Christlikeness as our goal has a lot of limits to it.

Most of us intuitively realize that being like Jesus and imitating him as his disciples means something, but that it doesn't mean those superficialities. For example, I've never known of a church discipleship program that sold first-century Jewish clothing. So what are some of the ways in which the goal of being like Jesus can be helpful, and what are its limits? [116]

When I played basketball through middle and high school and into college, my hero was David Robinson of the San Antonio Spurs. In my desire to imitate him, I wore his number 50 for as many seasons as I could. I was tall, and played the same position as he did. But being the tall kid, wearing number 50, and playing center didn't give me a stellar career like his. He had huge muscles, was incredibly quick for his size, could seemingly jump over opponents, and led the league in scoring, once scoring seventy-one points in a single game. My frame was skin and bones, I could reach nearly as high by standing as jumping, some other players could run backwards faster than I could at a sprint, and I averaged double points for each of my two college seasons (as in two points per game). But at least I wore David Robinson's number.

I still have great admiration for him, but my efforts to imitate David Robinson did not involve his abiding in me, and therefore, there certainly was no David Robinson stepping into my flesh and teaching me to play basketball from the inside out.

Imitation of Christ is irreplaceable in our lives as his disciples, yet the process of grace growing me into becoming truly and fully who I am in Christ does not consist solely of our efforts at imitation. Rather, this kind of life's foundation is the immense grace of Christ *in* me.

Jesus is absolutely my teacher, my savior, my example, and a long list of other titles. But striving to imitate anyone else's life—even *his*—can cause me to miss the grace of God that is uniquely and abundantly available in this life that God has given to *me*.

Perhaps another way to say it is like this: feel free to stop striving so hard to be *like* Jesus, and instead allow yourself to restfully yet resolutely abide *in* Christ, and allow Christ to abide *in* you. Then, though of course a vine and a branch are not the same thing, there won't be any way to draw a dividing line between the life of one and the life of the other.

"You have died, and your life is hidden with Christ in God. When Christ who is your life is revealed, then you also will be revealed with him in glory."[117]

As we have discussed in previous chapters, if grace is to take its full effect on any of us, it doesn't do so with us in isolation, but we need to give one another space, help, and support. We must encourage this kind of grace-full lifestyle in one another.

An often-misunderstood quote of John Wesley is, "no holiness but social holiness."[118] While Wesley was certainly adamant about our need to engage society as agents of change (which we focus on in the final chapter), that statement was not addressing the need for social activism. Rather, he was describing the necessity of involving others in our efforts to live holy lives. The fuller emphatic statement from Wesley is, "Holy solitaries is a phrase no more consistent with the gospel than holy adulterers. The gospel of Christ knows of no religion but social; no holiness but social holiness."[119]

The next chapter will focus more fully on this relational dynamic of our growth by grace. As the first step before we more fully turn the corner toward issues of community, I want to describe an important way that individual Christians for centuries have involved others in their efforts to become truly and fully who they are in Christ. This kind of relationship, which is devoted with specific attention to your life with God, is known as *spiritual direction*.

The name itself can convey some misguided ideas about what a spiritual direction relationship is, thinking that it will involve someone telling me what to do on spiritual things (as if to say, "Go home, read Habakkuk three times, and call me in the morning"). But rather than having a narrow focus on religious practices with the director being very directive like that, the focus of spiritual direction is on an individual's whole life and God's activity in it. Therefore, I think it is helpful to continue to use the same term as those in centuries before us, but to emphasize that the role of spiritual director is to *direct my attention to the work of the Holy Spirit in my life.*

Albert Haase says spiritual direction "is about committing to the attention, discovery and articulation of...the reality of God's grace in our lives,"[120] and he lists the following seven motivations for why someone might commit to sharing their life with God with a spiritual director:

- To learn how to be attentive to God's grace in one's life
- To deepen awareness of God's grace
- To explore what obstructs one's attention to God's grace
- To name and honor near occasions of grace
- To find the grace offered in loss, grief, anger, or fear
- To be conscious of God's grace in a moment of transition
- To make an important decision in light of God's grace

This helps to highlight the distinctions between meeting with a spiritual director and meeting with a therapist or pastoral counselor. While each of these relationships can be important and helpful, the focus is different. Therapeutic or counseling relationships are typically problem-centered. I might seek to engage a counselor for help with an issue: dealing with grief, relational difficulties, or anxiety, for example. I will probably meet with a counselor while I am dealing with the respective issue, and then—hopefully—come to a significant degree of healing in regard to it, and the therapy or counseling would end.

In spiritual direction, the focus is not on a particular problem, but on your life with God. Since they are not problem-centered, spiritual direction relationships can be longer-term, allowing us the immensely valuable experience of being known over time by someone who is prayerfully paying attention to us and to God as we meet together.

Spiritual direction primarily happens in one-on-one relationships between an individual and a trained spiritual director, although spiritual direction groups also exist and can also be a wonderful setting in which to allow others to participate in our journey.

A spiritual director sees the grace imbued in the directee's life, has experience in what it's like to stay planted, and is aware of the challenges involved in the growth process. Then the director is able to take that experience-based knowledge, prayerfully listen to our stories, and "name and honor the occasions of grace" within the realities of our lives.

The Jewish Talmud has a teaching which puts a powerful image on how a spiritual director's presence in our lives can help to stir the spark of God's grace in us: "Every blade of grass has its angel that bends over it and whispers, 'Grow, grow.'"[121]

———

Practice

- During some time in solitude this week, take some time to imagine your life fully grace-cooperative. What does that look like for you?

  Be careful to imagine it within the realities and limits of the life you've actually been given—meaning, if you're married, don't imagine yourself becoming a monk, etc. God's grace is abundantly available within your actual life, and at times we need to consider what it would practically look and feel like to entrust ourselves to God as fully as we know how.

  Perhaps you might find it helpful to focus your prayerful reflection around Gordon T. Smith's four invitations: what could wisdom, good work, love, and joy look like in my life?

- Consider meeting with a spiritual director. It may feel daunting to think about trying to find someone with whom to share your life with God in that way, but if you desire to do so, you can trust that God will help you. Trained spiritual directors are often available at retreat centers, monasteries, or seminaries. Also, technology is making it much easier to meet with a spiritual director who may not be in your area.

- Visit www.salvationlife.com/spiritual-direction/ for information on ways that I and others I know are currently involved in spiritual direction.
- CenterQuest (www.cqcenterquest.org) offers a Spiritual Direction Referral Network, with recommended directors from various Christian traditions.
- Spiritual Directors International (www.sdiworld.org) is an interfaith organization which has a worldwide listing of members.
- Or, feel free to email me at daniel@salvationlife.com, and I'll be happy to help you find a next step.

Eight

GRACE TO THE CHURCH

*I give you a new commandment, that you love one another. Just as I have
loved you, you also should love one another. By this everyone will know that
you are my disciples, if you have love for one another.*
John 13:34-35

*The Church is called holy, because it is holy, because every member thereof is
holy, though in different degrees, as He that called them is holy.*[122]
John Wesley

The Church is for discipleship. Discipleship is for the world.[123]
Dallas Willard

IF I AM GIVEN A WONDERFUL GIFT but misunderstand its
purpose, I am certain to get frustrated with it. Let's say that
someone gives me the world's greatest toaster as a gift. I
may have a general understanding that toasters heat food, and
for all of my life I have really enjoyed warm meals, so
therefore I feel a noticeable degree of excitement.

Perhaps I have a small frozen pizza which needs to be
heated and I am eager to utilize my newly gifted toaster. After
cramming the pizza into the slot on the toaster, turning it on
and waiting, I feel a noticeable degree of disappointment. The
pizza is indeed warm, but all of the cheese slid off the top.
After burning my hand in an attempt to recover my cheese-
loss, I conclude that the cheese is irretrievable. I also surmise
that all of the hype about toasters which I've heard my entire
life is another example of bogus marketing, and I resolve that I

will never again voluntarily put another morsel of food in one of these faulty contraptions.

Yes, the toaster is intended to heat food, but if we are trying to get a warm snack without the fuller picture of the appliance's purpose, we will not be able to cooperate with the gift given to us.

So it is also with the wonderful and sometimes painful means of God's grace known as *church*. Practically everyone who has ever been part of a church has come looking for the spiritual version of a warm and tasty snack. This is appropriate, particularly considering that Jesus' instruction to the first leader of his church was, "feed my lambs."[124] Yet it isn't the full picture.

As many churches do, the one my family attends takes this feeding aspect literally and seriously. When we walk in the doors on Sunday mornings, food greets us. There is coffee, juice, water, donuts, fruit, and—yes—warm, toasty and tasty snacks. But what happens when the snack tables are cleared and the food put away? Do we suddenly become less able to do the kinds of things Jesus said to do?

My term for this first stage of church is *Feed Me*. We come to church because of its benefits, which usually go beyond the actual edible snacks. Maybe the music is great. Maybe the preaching inspires us. Maybe it's fun to see friends there each week. Maybe it just makes us feel better when we go.

The number of ways that grace can stir us in this stage is limitless, but all of this kind of food inevitably has an expiration date. One of the most common reasons I have heard for folks changing churches is, "I'm just not being fed here anymore." Maybe the music changes. Maybe the preaching that once inspired you starts to sound the same week after week. Maybe they started substituting cheaper coffee for the good stuff. For church to be the lifelong means of grace into you and me that it is intended to be, we have to realize that the expiration date on the snacks is part of the process, because a lifetime in the *Feed Me* stage is incapable of teaching us to deny ourselves, take up our crosses, and genuinely follow our ancient Jewish rabbi.

———

Some folks never get beyond this stage of church. To stay stuck there either requires a good bit of church-swapping through one's life, or just dropping out. If you and I stay past the time when the snacks are what draw us in, grace will do its work, plant us a little deeper, and lead us to put a foot on the next rung down on the ladder into the hole where we are planted: *Give Me a Place to Serve*.

If we came into church with a misguided idea of its purpose, it will probably require some wise guidance from another person to help us put a foot down tentatively one step deeper. Ideally that guidance could come from memories of our own parents' involvement in church, though it could come from anyone who has stayed planted before us. Regardless of the source, the grace-catalyst for the transition will be a combination of the expiration date on the snacks and a realization something like: "Oh...they learned other ways to be fed. For them, participating in church wasn't really about being fed, but about serving others."

This second stage often involves a wonderfully liberating experience of coming to know with more clarity how God wired us, particularly by discovering and employing our gifts for the sake of others. Whether it is an artistic talent and appreciation for beauty, a natural ability for administration, an ease in making others feel welcome or loved, a passion to work to correct injustices, a love of learning and teaching, a capacity to organize and motivate others, an enjoyment of using technical skills, or that you are an all-around ultimate team player willing to do whatever needs to be done—or any of a long list of other possibilities—it is a joy to discover that you have abilities that can play an important part in serving others in and through the church. The feeling of really coming alive while serving others with gifts that are genuinely yours is an invaluable experience of grace taking its effect on you.

Folks can genuinely and appropriately stay in this stage for a long time. Although it doesn't last forever, there is no specific time limit here, and as long as it remains a the rung which most feels like home to us—and most continues to stir God's grace in us—engagement in it is to be encouraged. Indeed, even once we have stepped down to the third rung on the ladder, we still have one foot in this stage. The shape of the invitation to serve others in ways congruent with our wiring and life circumstances can change over time, but the invitation itself always remains a practical part of what it means to be Jesus' disciple.

———

The transition from this rung down to the third one on the ladder of our being planted more deeply can be tricky, and is often painful. It might be that over time we came to employ our gifts and talents in ways that became compulsive, rather than genuine expressions of love. Maybe we burn out, or maybe our favorite way to serve is no longer asked for. Whatever the impetus for the shift is, it often feels like involuntarily hitting some kind of wall.[125] This is the point when we most need a clear understanding of the gift's purpose and some wise guidance to help us continue to cooperate with grace and stay planted.

Folks who didn't drop out during the first transition may do so during this one unless there is an unusually high degree of understanding of the overall process and how and why grace takes us through these stages. Once again, gaining that understanding requires some wise guidance, but the direction given can help lead us to an invaluable commitment to something which our culture generally does not esteem: *stability*.

Hitting the wall makes us want to pull back from all of the ways that we had been engaged. Although there is wisdom in having rhythms of disengagement in our lives, the disengagement itself is not necessarily a form of cooperating with grace, any more than doing its opposite and jumping into a flurry of activity automatically would be. Having someone to accompany us on the journey as a spiritual director or close spiritual friend is always valuable, and at this point it is nearly a necessity in the process of becoming truly and fully who we are in Christ in the context of our relationships with others in the church. Otherwise, hitting the wall can easily lead us to withdraw all the way out of the hole in which we have been planted. Even if we don't drop out, we may stay around with constant and growing cynicism and bitterness combined with reduced emotional engagement. The very devotion to our churches which previously fueled our engagement can become twisted, leading us along a path of spiritual malformation rather than continued transformation, so that we become cancers within these fellowships we formerly sought to enliven. Both clergy and laity are at risk of this.

When we hit the wall, it does not feel like an occasion of grace. In fact, the wall may have been constructed from our well-intentioned but misguided efforts and choices—such as if our years in the *Feed Me* and *Give Me a Place to Serve* stages were at least as motivated by our own ego and unmet needs as they were directed by the Spirit of the living, loving God. This is not fun to realize. But whether it is a realization like that, or something equivalent that stuns us, we simply feel incapable of continuing in our old, familiar ways.

Though the wall itself may not have been constructed of 100% grace-cooperative efforts, when we hit it, we can experience the stillness which it demands of us, and do what we can to remain open to God and others even while we lie there at its base. Slow and surprising signs of grace can emerge even while we are still dealing with the bruises we just incurred in our collision.

My own wall experience was both crushing and grace-laden like this. I had been working on staff in churches and ministries for fourteen years. As I look back on it now, the wall had been creeping up on me for a long time, but I tried to ignore it and pretend it wouldn't matter to me—as if I would somehow blaze my own trail around it or miraculously march right through it. I have a lot of good memories from those fourteen years, and a lot of painful ones. I can now see how much of my wall was built from years of efforts of trying to be someone I was not in order to do jobs I thought were important and meet others' expectations of me. There was no ill-will in any of this—I was serving the best I knew how, and people in those churches often wanted/needed a certain kind of person in their stated or unstated goals, and over time it became more and more apparent that I was mismatched for that kind of leadership. Dismissing that for so long sucked the life out of me.

About the same time that I was at my most debilitated and depleted point in those leadership roles, my father—who had been my hero throughout my life—was diagnosed with cancer and died six months later. I had faced difficult situations before, but that was the first time when I had absolutely no idea how to handle what life was throwing at me. The combination of my depletion and my grief over my dad left me feeling completely unable to function. I had smacked into the wall which had been growing on my horizon for so long, and it felt like I could do nothing except lay there and hurt. Continuing along the course I had been taking for so long was impossible.

It was following my crumpling experience at that wall that I began to lean into some of the practices I had been studying, teaching, and dabbling in for years—like solitude and silence, plus spiritual direction to help me process it all. By God's grace, I found myself in a community of other ministry leaders who were exploring these practices together. I described some of my experiences of hitting the wall to our community's teacher, who responded, "You need to go underground."[126]

I needed to stop flailing around, and learn to just stay planted. In an ironic twist, since the wall was constructed in part from so many of my own well-intentioned but misguided efforts, after I crashed into it one of the things I needed to learn most from it was to imitate its stillness. I needed to let grace take me another step deeper in my planting. Allowing this let me experience a taste of the true purpose of the gift of the church, as I moved into its third stage: *Teach Me to Love*.

———

Lying there bruised after hitting the wall following so many years of giving so much of my best effort to church, I really didn't expect that my own church would be the next major (and desperately needed) means of grace for me. It would slowly lead to me being able to dust myself off and attempt to follow God into a different way of living and directing my efforts.

Over the years of being in different roles as an associate minister in churches, I didn't always handle difficult relationships in church well, and that was particularly troublesome in the times when those difficult relationships were between me and any of the senior pastors I worked with, who were all very dedicated to the church and their roles within it. However, one grace-laden relationship stands out for me for which I will always be grateful. Over the time I worked with one pastor, it became apparent that we viewed some fundamental parts of my role in the church's ministry differently, and this led to some difficult conversations. For the rest of my life, I will be grateful for how my pastor handled that, and how he allowed me to handle it. He gave me the space to disagree with him, regardless of the size of the issues, and for us to continue to love one another. We were committed to loving each other, and because of that, we knew we were safe with one another.

In this instance—because Jesus' instruction of loving each other was our supreme value—we were able to give each other space, to extend grace to one another, and I am absolutely better off because of it. It helped me become more truly and fully who I am in Christ and—eventually—to make a more helpful and genuine contribution to the church.

> *To disagree, but continue to genuinely love one another is an important part of the ongoing work of God's grace, and it only happens with stability.*

To disagree, but continue to genuinely love one another is an important part of the ongoing work of God's grace, and it only happens with stability. Loving each other like that is central to what it means for the church to be the church—which can stir the spark of God's grace in us in ways that nothing else can.

Churches and Health Clubs

A number of years ago, my wife and I gave the first of our multiple attempts to become regular exercisers at the local YMCA. We had been talking for a long time about the need to be healthier, but had yet to do any of the necessary things to see it happen. So one day, we felt particularly motivated, went in to join and paid the first month's membership fee.

A staff member gave us a tour of the facility on our joining day, and it was difficult to not feel out of place. I was the most out of shape I had ever been, but on our tour I saw plenty of people sweating profusely and enjoying it. People (expressly meaning both men and women) were lifting weights so heavy that when the bar went back on the rack, I could feel the floor shaking and reverberating through my legs. Sure, there were also plenty of people there in a physical condition much closer to mine, but I didn't take as much notice of them.

While it felt intimidating in a way, there was also certainly a sense of it being right. If we had walked around the facility without seeing anyone who looked healthy, there would be a serious problem. Health clubs don't exist just to get people to sign up—they are there to help people get healthy.

Pause those thoughts about a health club for a moment and think about a church. I once heard Dallas Willard say that we need to stop counting the people who come to our churches and start weighing them.[127] Obviously he wasn't advocating that we place scales around our churches. Rather, he was making the point that the number of people who come is only relevant if they are reliably growing in Christ in the substance of who they are—if they are cooperating with grace and more truly and fully becoming who they are in Christ. Or, back to the health club, the number of members is irrelevant if no one there is getting healthy. (Or we could easily go back to our seed metaphor: a nursery that had a few thousand trees would be useless if none of them—or even just a minority of them— were growing.)

Although a health club would probably go out of business if it was a rarity to have members become and stay healthy, it can take a long time for the momentum of a church to die out, even if it is not focused on the best things. It is possible to have a church of any size whose people do not regularly become more Christlike as time passes. Churches can make the *Feed Me* or *Give Me a Place to Serve* stage their specialty, and actually discourage folks from moving beyond either one. The folks in the church can work hard, do everything with excellence, be extremely well-organized with strong leadership at all levels— and if those components are in place, chances are that a church in the culture where I live will not have trouble drawing a crowd. Yet even if folks are consistently being fed and/or serving, those characteristics are not identical with whether or not people in the church are increasing their capacity for love of God and others.

The aim is to build bigger Christians, which is not necessarily the same thing as building bigger churches. Surely some health clubs get this right. They exist to help people get fit, and if they do that extremely well, I doubt they have trouble finding business. If I were a health club director, my primary goal would be to get as many people as possible onto a reliable path to getting and staying fit. So, in terms of the church, that means to get as many people as possible to enter ever more fully into "the life that really is life," leading them in the kind of lifestyle in which God will naturally produce the love, joy, and peace of Christ deep within them as they learn to rely on and cooperate with grace.

> *One of our greatest unrecognized desperations is for our pastors to experience full and deeply satisfying lives in Christ, because they cannot lead us where they have not gone.*

It also means that we need to be serious about supporting and encouraging our pastors in every way possible so that they can truly and fully become who *they* are in Christ. One of our greatest unrecognized desperations is for our pastors to experience full and deeply satisfying lives in Christ, because they cannot lead us where they have not gone. We need to have a tremendous deal of compassion for the very difficult work they do, and take any opportunity that presents itself to encourage them.

I suppose that health clubs can run successfully as businesses without fit directors, though that seems difficult. Pastors, on the other hand, can conceivably build big churches without having had their characters transformed to be very significantly like that of Jesus—yet I don't know how we can build "big" Christians without having grown very "big" ourselves. In fact, without Christ's character growing in us through God's grace, we likely won't even know what it would mean to make "bigger Christians" and may not even recognize them if we met one. Leadership inevitably involves influencing others to become like us, so building bigger Christians requires those in Christian leadership to themselves be apprentices of Jesus, learning to do everything he taught us. So may we always love and encourage our pastors—because we depend on them, our churches depend on them, our cities depend on them, and—really—our world depends on them.

Maybe I'm giving health clubs too much credit. I'm sure they also occasionally fall into the trap of focusing on expanding their customer base without giving the needed attention to how effectively they're helping the people who are already there to become healthy. If that's true, the largest health club in town is not necessarily the one most likely to help you get in shape. And equivalently, the largest church is not automatically the place that can most effectively give you the space for grace to take you through these three stages as you remain planted along with the others in that orchard. The orchard can be large or small. Size is not the point. The point is bigger Christians, not bigger churches.[128]

If, as we said in the previous chapter, wholeness—or holiness, or maturity in Christ—is our goal, then the church's goal is to help people move—from wherever they are and whichever stage is home to them at the moment—in the direction of wholeness/holiness/maturity. To mix our seed and health club metaphors, we could say that the church's goal is to help people, at whatever size they are, to get bigger. (That could make for some great advertising: "Come to our church and we'll help you add some girth." Maybe even change the church's name to Girth Community Church.)

———

This is implicit in what we have explored above, but it needs to be said again more explicitly here: If we are to truly and fully become who we are in Christ, we *cannot* do it alone. As we explored in chapter two, pecan trees do not come to their full pecan-ness in isolation, nor can you and I become truly and fully who we are in Christ without involving other people in our growth. It doesn't happen any other way, because we human beings are simply not designed for it to happen any other way.

Stephen Neill describes this well:

> *If I am called to be a saint, if I am really expected to be so much like Jesus Christ that others will know at once and unmistakably that I am a Christian, then . . . I shall need all the help that I can possibly get. I know that I cannot climb this hill by myself; I shall need at every point the help, the encouragement, the understanding of those who have valiantly set themselves to climb it too.*[129]

We find this help from others on the same journey in each of these three stages, as well as the crucial transitions between them. In the *Feed Me* stage, others around us do the feeding, plus it's fun to enjoy being fed well alongside others. Then we receive guidance as we put a step down further, and again we need others in the *Give Me a Place to Serve* stage.

Then, of course, others are the core of the experience in the *Teach Me to Love* stage. Second to our families, church should be the central place where we learn to love. We aren't often trained to think of church in this way—especially about the hard relationships in church. Usually, if we are involved enough in the church to come into a hard relationship (and every one of us will—because churches are full of human beings), we tend to view those as exceptions to what church is supposed to be rather than being a *central and irreplaceable part of the curriculum of the church.* When a church relationship gets difficult, we start thinking, "Oh this isn't how church is supposed to be! We're all supposed to be loving here!" Well, yes, we are—and *that* difficult relationship is one of the primary teachers regarding how to fulfill Jesus' commandment: love one another.

As grace grows me while I stay planted and I experience the wonder of Christ abiding in me, along the way I will also realize that Christ likewise abides in these brothers and sisters of mine with whom I sing these songs and hear these stories each Sunday. Eventually we come to realize that the last commandment of the Christ who dwells in both of us is not, "Do all things in church with excellence! Or you're fired!" Nor is it, "Do as much activity for my sake as possible!" Rather, it is, "Love each other as I have loved you." Seeing Christ in the other trees growing in this orchard alongside me transforms the conflicts that will come along from being exceptions to how things are supposed to be into being expected growing pains in this process of—together—becoming truly and fully who we are in Christ.

––––––

Practice

Although I have sought to describe our experience in church in these stages, I do not mean to imply that anyone should be in any stage other than the one where they really are at the moment. In that light, take some time to reflect honestly about your experience in church by writing a timeline of your significant church experiences, whether positive or negative, and however few or many they may be. This may lead you to express a lot of gratitude as memories surface, or it might take more of the form of a complaint, or some of both. It may describe something of your experience in the different stages from this chapter. Whatever form it takes, your goal in writing this is to enable you to say something as honest as you can to God about your experience with church.

Then (because this is ultimately about experience, rather than ideas), contact someone whose life with God you admire and ask if you can share your timeline with them. This may take place within an existing relationship of spiritual direction or spiritual friendship, or in a different setting, but your goal in sharing your honest reflection is to experience the unique way that two trees staying planted in the same orchard over time can play a role in one another's growth in grace (in other words, to experience church).

Nine

GRACE TO THE WORLD

The creation waits with eager longing
for the revealing of the children of God.
Romans 8:19

[Those who] fear God, and desire the happiness of their fellow-creatures,
have, in every age, found it needful to join together, in order to oppose the
works of darkness, to spread the knowledge of God their Saviour, and to
promote his kingdom upon earth.[130]
John Wesley

There is a way of life that, if generally adopted, would eliminate all of the
social and political problems from which we suffer. This way of life comes to
whole-hearted disciples of Christ who live in the disciplines of the spiritual life
and allow grace to bring their bodies into alignment with their spirits.[131]
Dallas Willard

E VERY ONCE IN A WHILE, if I am looking for them, I
encounter statements which feel as if within just a few
words, they are able to explain at least eighty percent of
what my mind has been wrestling with for years. That has
happened for me a number of times with Wesley and Willard,
and it has also been the case at times digging into the writings
of M. Robert Mulholland. Primary among Mulholland's
staggering statements for me is when he says that often we
"will expend amazing amounts of energy and resources to be
in the world for God. But, you see, we are called to be in God
for the world."[132]

I feel astounded again even as I just re-read and typed his sentence here, because those twenty-eight words seem to explain decades of my life.

When I crashed into the wall I described in the previous chapter and one of my teachers wisely told me, "you need to go underground," she was pointing to the same dynamic as Mulholland's words. I had expended a lot of energy trying to be in the world for God, and I was utterly depleted. The invitation at hand, about which I both felt fear and longing, was to allow everything to be pruned except learning to live my life in God and to submit any results of my existence in this world to the steadfastly loving Father of Jesus rather than to the work roles I had engaged in for God's sake for so long.

So, I am remarkably well-acquainted with the first half of Mulholland's statement (the well-intentioned but misguided living in the world for God), and my hope is to spend the rest of my life as an experiment in the second part (living in God for the world). My experience of going underground and of learning to stay planted for the long haul has given me occasional, small tastes of what "in God for the world" means. The central lesson perhaps seems obvious but in practice is very counter-intuitive: arranging our lives to be lived fully in God is the only way that we can become carriers of the incomparable gift of God's grace to the world.

To make this a bit more practical: I need solitude (aloneness with God) in order to be able to genuinely encounter others and love them well, rather than unconsciously seeking to manipulate them for my own satisfaction. I need silence (quietness with God) in order to be able to recognize when the words I say to another person are coming from an honest, open, loving place within me or when they are trying to impress, cajole, or otherwise control the person to whom I say them. I need to learn all of the seemingly unproductive practices of cooperating with grace, because a lifetime and lifestyle of staying planted through them is the only way that any fruit from my life will be a grace-result and not my own counterfeit production.

This is every bit as true, practical, and applicable for bankers, teachers, movie stars, janitors, lawyers, business leaders, students, pastors, aid workers, and politicians as it is for monks and retreat leaders. Grace is lavishly available in each of our lives, as well as sufficient time for us to cooperate with it. We have to be intentional about looking for the opportunities to do the kinds of grace-cooperating practices we have explored in this book, and we must be vigilant not to waste those opportunities as they are naturally given to us. For the sake of the world (including spouses, parents, or children living within our own homes as well as refugees and sex-trafficking victims on the other side of the globe), it is imperative that we learn to live in God and allow grace to have its maximum impact on us so that the grace-parched world around us can find some relief. As Mulholland also says, "we become either agents of God's healing and liberating grace or carriers of the sickness of the world."[133]

The tricky thing about all of this is that it is so easy for me to deceive myself. I can talk myself into thinking that I am living in God for the world and therefore becoming an agent of God's grace, when my motivations are really coming from many things other than God's life and love. So I end up spreading my own sickness while convincing myself I've been doing a lot of things in the world for God. I don't think Mulholland's words will ever cease to be a challenging reminder for me. God is not interested in you or me doing things in the world for anyone's sake (not even God's own), but we are given the incomprehensibly good invitation to draw our lives from God so that we can become whatever kind of benefit for the world that God determines.

———

I first read those statements from Dr. Mulholland as part of his exploration of a parable Jesus told along these lines which can either be read as chilling or liberating.[134] Near the end of the Sermon on the Mount, Jesus says,

> Not everyone who says to me, "Lord, Lord," will enter the kingdom of heaven, but only the one who does the will of my Father in heaven. On that day many will say to me, "Lord, Lord, did we not prophesy in your name, and cast out demons in your name, and do many deeds of power in your name?" Then I will declare to them, "I never knew you; go away from me, you evildoers."[135]

Perhaps on the first reading, that passage might seem to lean more toward the chilling side of things than the liberating, but I think it can be either. I felt it to be very liberating at a time when I was only about a couple of years into being in full-time ministry. However long the exact time had been, it was long enough that I was beginning to realize that my hopes for what my ministry would be like were completely inaccurate. I was a youth minister at the time, and I thought that I would have teenagers flocking to what we were doing, new kids would be coming to faith all the time, and parents of the teenagers would consistently love me and my work. The reality was not anywhere near my expectations.

Somewhere during that time, I remember reading this parable from the Sermon on the Mount, and I felt released by the perspective it gave me. I realized that I had received a wealth of valuable training on how to build a great ministry, how to help people know Jesus, and how to impact the world for God. The education was inspiring, and I am still grateful to have had it, but I was deeply disappointed that those results were not happening.

Although I hadn't previously seen my experience in the context of Jesus' parable, I came to realize that I had *really* wanted to be one of the people he was describing, often more interested in results than a relationship. I would have even settled for significantly less dramatic results than in the parable, but seriously—if I could have prophesied, cast out demons, and done many deeds of power in Jesus' name, I would have been a huge ministry success story (and a *remarkably* humble one, of course). Instead of a success story, my ministry efforts to that point felt much more like a painfully long run on a treadmill—working hard but going nowhere.

That was when the liberating invitation came. The parable indicated that Jesus was not demanding ministry results from me, nor is he now demanding them of you. God wants to *know* us. Christ wants to abide in us, and us in him.

If you have ever wished that you could have the kind of impact for God in the world that you've seen someone else have (and I am saying this as someone who has done so—and still does—more often than I can admit easily to myself or to any of you), God does not want that from you. You have not failed to reach any "in the world for God" quota for your life. Jesus states emphatically that above all else, he wants to know you. The genuine "produce" from our lives comes from that personal knowledge. Any fruit produced from another source is dangerous, inevitably spreading something other than grace.

The expectations we put on ourselves and our desire to see results cause us to prematurely over-strategize our efforts to do good in the world. Although the intentions often spring from an honest motivation to do God's will, there's also a more subtle desire to shortcut the process in favor of quicker results. We want so badly to produce the fruit, and just letting ourselves stay planted in the conditions conducive to grace continuing to grow us feels like a colossal waste of time. (*Because just think of all of the things I could be doing in the world for God if I wasn't stuck in this hole!*)

We see an area in which we think that things can be accomplished for God, and we want to jump right into the action. We so quickly forget examples such as the energetic and highly-driven Paul spending three years completely underground after encountering the risen Christ on the road to Damascus, before he ever taught anyone anything about the Messiah. Jesus himself spent thirty years *not* doing ministry— not preaching, not doing any miracles, just living his life with his family and learning to fully be who he was.

When our lives stay planted in this way, practically and meaningfully entrusting our existence and the results of our efforts to God, then any visible results that may or may not come from our lives are up to God, not to us. It is only people who are learning to live like that who can freely offer God's gift of grace to the world, without tainting it with our own ambitions.

———

It is difficult for me to write a chapter like this, because I am well aware that one of my own stumbling blocks is a deeply ingrained bias toward reflection over action. For example, I recently participated in a chapel service which involved each of us going to an altar and lighting a candle. The person in front of me lit their candle put it in its place, and then knelt to pray. After they closed their eyes in prayer, I noticed their candle tilting forward, touching some fabric on the altar, and catching it on fire. Instead of doing the obviously needed thing and *acting*, I stood there *thinking*: "Wow, that flame is already pretty big. I don't think blowing on it will be sufficient. I can't put it out with my hand. I wish I had read a book on how to deal with altar flames...." My mental processes were interrupted by our group's leader noticing the inactive look on my face, rushing over, blowing out the flame and pouring some water on it for good measure. I thank God that most people are more action-oriented than I am, or we would probably all have been engulfed in the flames by now.

I tell that story for the benefit of those of you who know me well enough to perhaps have seen some of my bias toward inaction in between the lines of the paragraphs above. Regardless of how valid of a caution that may be, I am convinced that it is a mistake to think of "in the world for God" as meaning that things will get done, while "in God for the world" (along with the silence, solitude, and other practices of staying planted which I'm advocating) means that we will be too contemplative to accomplish anything. Rather, every one of us—from the speedy to the slow-poke—can learn a way of living (including both reflecting and acting) which opens us and allows God's grace to go through us to the world, uninhibited and actually enriched by the endless variety of creative personalities we carry in the world as children of our Creator.

The outcomes of staying planted for me will look very different than they will for you. For example, one of the things that opened up for me as I went underground was to discover how important writing is for my own continuing soul-work, and how I can make a more genuine contribution to the church through it than through the administration at which I used to try to force myself to reach an average performance level. I need to keep writing things like the pages in this book as part of the process of continuing to become who I am in Christ, regardless of who does or does not read them. For you, it will be something else.

For example, I know of a group of medical doctors whose process of staying planted stirred a desire in them to move into rough areas of Memphis as "a community of Christian disciples using health strategies to restore spiritual, physical and social well being among the world's most marginalized by developing leaders and providing compassionate care."[136]

I know of a group of lawyers, activists, and law enforcement officials who seek to address the immense problem of poverty by dealing with what they have identified as its primary sustaining factor: the threat of violence which the poor face in everyday life. In the midst of the unending nature of their work, they make a practice of pausing in silence for thirty minutes each day, as a part of their work together, because of their desire to do their jobs from their connection to Christ.[137]

This commitment to staying planted and learning to live our lives in God for the world is a commitment to flooding the world with God's grace, because it is the way in which we intentionally learn to align our efforts with what God is doing in the world.

————

In the various things that you and I will do today, we inevitably have some degree of say over how things will go. We have surely learned by now that there is much of what happens which we cannot control, but nonetheless, each of us has a range of things in which our desires shape what happens. On one end of the scale, that range is small for young children, and on the other end, it is very large for the person who holds the highest office in a nation. Regardless of how large or small that range is, this is true for you, and Dallas Willard describes this as your kingdom. God has a kingdom, so do you and I, and I seek to live in cooperation with grace so that my kingdom can come into line with God's. I want to live in this staying-planted kind of way so that "thy kingdom come, thy will be done, on earth as it is in heaven" can move from only

> *I want to live in this staying-planted kind of way so that "thy kingdom come, thy will be done, on earth as it is in heaven" can move from only being a plea that God would make something happen to giving God a life through which it can.*

being a plea that God would make something happen to giving God a life through which it can.

Willard says,

> *Things will go right in human life and society only to the extent that a sufficient number of qualified people are adequately distributed and positioned to see to it that they go right. Justice cannot prevail until there are enough people properly equipped with Christ's character and power...who cooperatively and under God constantly see to it that the good is secured and that the right is done...Only then will brotherhood, justice, well-being, and, consequently, peace prevail upon the earth. Is this possible? I don't believe it's a mere dream or a desperate delusion, once we understand how the disciplines mesh with grace, on the one hand, and embodied human personality, on the other.*[138]

If you and I are to stay planted for the long haul, leaving ourselves in the conditions that will allow grace to grow us into being fully and truly who we are in Christ, we must believe those words are possible. We must believe that we can better engage and love those around us when we have rhythms of being alone with God, developing our attentiveness to God through prayer, and renewing our hearts and minds through reading the Scriptures. We must believe that cultivating our lives in God as disciples of Jesus matters for the sake of the world, or else we will never be able to fully give ourselves over to the process.

But, as is always the case, telling ourselves that we must believe something doesn't do anything to make us actually believe it. Today, as you finish this final chapter of this book, I invite you to experiment and see for yourself whether or not this kind of life works. If you give yourself over to it as fully as you know how, through the kinds of thinking, practices, and relationships that we have explored, find out whether or not God will meet you, guide you, and grow you by grace into truly and fully who you are in Christ.

Practice

We often tend to think of doing God's will as the kind of stuff we chart off years into our future. One of the pastors to whom this book is dedicated once taught me a much more helpful approach: "Make sure you're in God's will today. Then you won't miss it tomorrow."

Part A: Think over the next twenty-four hours, considering how you could be in God's will *today* / cooperate as fully with grace as you know how to do this day.

Part B: Then, tomorrow, spend a few minutes reflecting on whether or not giving yourself to God in this manner mattered for others.

Conclusion

WHEN MY CHILDREN WERE NEWBORNS, I *loved* them intensely, but the degree to which I *knew* them was limited by their infancy. When they were in diapers, my wife and I knew them better than anyone else on the planet, but we did not know them as completely as we do now that they can write, talk, and live in a maturing relationship with us. Our love for them has remained steadfast and strong, and although we have always been the two who have known them best, our ability to know them expands and deepens as they grow.

Not to your surprise—you are a *person*, rather than a pecan tree, and ultimately God gives this gift of grace that grows us so that you and I can grow into people ever more capable of knowing and being known by God.

Perhaps this addresses something that puzzled me for a long time in the parable of Jesus included in the last chapter from the Sermon on the Mount. Jesus said,

> Not everyone who says to me, 'Lord, Lord,' will enter the kingdom of heaven, but only the one who does the will of my Father in heaven. On that day many will say to me, 'Lord, Lord, did we not prophesy in your name, and cast out demons in your name, and do many deeds of power in your name?' Then I will declare to them, 'I never knew you; go away from me, you evildoers.'[139]

Jesus indicates that the intent was not ministry successes, but relationship—that he would have known them.

But how could he say he didn't know them? In the way I always thought of it, the passage should have said, "Then I will declare to them, '*You* never knew *me*", because clearly Jesus would have known them.

Maybe part of what the parable teaches us is that *as persons rather than pecan trees, grace grows us into ever-increasing capacity for knowing and being known.*

When you were the human equivalent of a seed in the ground, God loved you intensely and knew you better than anyone else, but as you have grown, God has known you increasingly and continued to love you strongly and steadfastly. God so generously gives this gift of grace that grows you because of the intense desire expressed by Jesus in the parable to *know you.*[140]

Perhaps—just as I feel like I need to do right now—the best way to respond to that is to find a quiet place, waste some time with this God who knows and loves you, and open yourself once again to this incredible gift of grace.

SUGGESTIONS FOR STAYING PLANTED

A NOTEWORTHY DANGER FOR PEOPLE LIKE ME is that of reading a book about life with God which inspires us, and to let that feeling be twisted so that we confuse the inspiration for actual growth. While putting good things into our minds is highly commendable in our efforts to cooperate with grace, reading a book about becoming truly and fully who I am in Christ is a very different thing that actually becoming able to show up in the world as that person.

The first suggestion for avoiding that danger is to *read this book with others*. Whether it is with a friend who also desires this kind of life or with a group in your community, the difference in processing ideas and practices like this with others as opposed to going through it alone is significant. One way of doing this would be to get together weekly, alternating weeks between discussing the content of a chapter, and then—the following week—to discuss your experiences with the corresponding practice session at the end of the respective chapter.

If the discussion of spiritual direction in Chapter Seven seemed inviting to you, another good way of continuing your journey by involving others in it would be to *connect with a spiritual director*. You may want to revisit the ways of connecting with a director mentioned in the Practice section at the end of that chapter.

A life-saving experience for me, which led me to begin to experiment with this kind of life and gave me relationships, teaching and support to continue in it, was my *participation in a Transforming Community*. The Transforming Community experience consists of two years of quarterly retreats focused on the strengthening the souls of pastors and Christian leaders, guided by the teaching of Ruth Haley Barton. For more information, see http://www.transformingcenter.org.

An introductory opportunity for connecting with others and exploring these practices which doesn't involve travel is to *participate in CenterQuest's online Lifelong Learning Community.* Various courses are offered each year on Christian Spirituality, including my own "Exploring the Prayerful Life: Developing a Lifestyle of Attentiveness to God." See a list of upcoming course offerings at: http://www.cqcenterquest.org/offerings-resources/cq-lifelong-learning-community/.

Finally, if you have shared your own journey with a spiritual director for some time and have a desire to explore accompanying others as they seek to become truly and fully who they are in Christ, I highly recommend *CenterQuest's School of Spiritual Direction*. See more information at http://www.cqcenterquest.org/school-of-spiritual-direction/.

GRATITUDES

The process of this book coming to exist has involved many more people than any other writing project of which I have been a part. Some have knowingly participated in the process, aware that they were helping me get a book into print. Many others have participated unknowingly—whether through attending a retreat or having a good conversation.

The content of the book is from a series of retreats I developed for the Spiritual Formation Center of First United Methodist Church of Midland, Texas. I am grateful to Tim Walker for allowing me the opportunity to develop those retreats over a number of years, and to the folks who have participated in the retreats along the way.

The following group of folks with whom I've had a variety of connections over time gave feedback on the project, which helped make the book better: Vanessa Caruso, Carol Ann Childlaw, Rick Enns, Pilar Ferrer, Tanya Francis, Jocelyn Furr, Cathy Harris, Greg Haseloff, Steve LaMotte, Susie Mason, Bill Mefford, Gretchen Roderick, Christy Swaringen, Tim Walker, and Kendon Wheeler. Ryan Bash and Robert Pelfrey are pastors and fellow writers whose insights on the content are always valuable and on whose friendship I have leaned heavily for a long time.

Since the book emphasizes the centrality of community in the process of becoming who we are in Christ, it's fitting that I mention the communities that have shaped me during the years this book has come together. I am involved in two communities specifically dedicated to the transformation of those of us who have participated: The Transforming Center, under the teaching of Ruth Haley Barton, and CenterQuest, where I was trained in Spiritual Direction and have benefited deeply from the leadership and friendship of Wil Hernandez. Since one way to describe the aim of this book is to explore the core of a Christian practice of spiritual formation, I was honored that Wil would write the foreword for the book because of how deeply his own ongoing "quest for the center" has affected me.

The next community is my church, First United Methodist Church of Midland, Texas. The ways I am fed, have opportunities to serve, and learn to love there are invaluable, and I am grateful to continue to explore this kind of life there alongside my pastor and friend, Steve Brooks.

The most central and enjoyable community is my family. Kara, Ethan, and Mia make me want to stay planted for the long haul and be the biggest, strongest tree I can be. In them is all my delight.

And one more note, about a couple of folks who feel like family to me: the tree on the cover image is not a pecan, but an old, giant oak at the home of Jim and Jerry Lee. They (and their oak) are an invaluable part of the process of me becoming truly and fully who I am in Christ.

ABOUT THE AUTHOR

Daniel Ethan Harris is a spiritual director, writer, and manages a family business in Midland, Texas. He can be contacted through SalvationLife.com.

His other books include:

- *Live Prayerfully: How Ordinary Lives Become Prayerful*
- *Follow: 40 Days of Preparing the Soul for Easter*
- *Wait: Four Weeks of Preparing the Soul for Christmas*
- *My Father in Me: Stories of My Dad's Life and How They've Shaped Who I Am* (an ebook available for free at SalvationLife.com)

Notes

[1] This framework was inspired by James Bryan Smith's triangle of "The Four Components of Transformation," which is central to all of the books in his Apprentice Series, and is introduced in "Chapter One: What Are You Seeking?" of his *The Good and Beautiful God: Falling in Love with the God Jesus Knows* (Downers Grove, IL: InterVarsity Press, 2009), 19-32.

[2] John Wesley, Sermon 79, "On Dissipation," section 1.20, in *The Sermons of John Wesley*, ed. Thomas Jackson, The Wesley Center for Applied Theology, accessed March 9, 2017, http://wesley.nnu.edu/john-wesley/the-sermons-of-john-wesley-1872-edition/sermon-79-on-dissipation/.

[3] Dallas Willard, *The Great Omission: Reclaiming Jesus' Essential Teachings on Discipleship* (New York: HarperCollins, 2006), 62.

[4] I heard Dallas say this verbally. A printed statement that comes close is, "Grace: God acting in our life to bring about, and to enable us to do, what we cannot do on our own. (2 Tim. 2:1) Grace is for whole life and not just for forgiveness."

From "Willard Words," http://www.dwillard.org/resources/willardwords.asp, accessed April 19, 2017.

[5] Willard, "How Does a Disciple Live?," *dwillard.org,* accessed March 9, 2017, http://www.dwillard.org/articles/artview.asp?artID=103.

[6] Romans 5:20-21.

[7] Smith, *The Good and Beautiful God*, 102.

[8] See Matthew chapter 6.

[9] Daniel Ethan Harris, "My Bad Christmas Prayer Idea," *SalvationLife.com*, published December 27, 2012, http://www.salvationlife.com/blog/2012/12/27/my-bad-christmas-prayer-idea.

[10] John Wesley, Sermon 43, "The Scripture Way of Salvation," section 3.1, in *The Sermons of John Wesley*, ed. Thomas Jackson, The Wesley Center for Applied Theology, accessed March 9, 2017, http://wesley.nnu.edu/john-wesley/the-sermons-of-john-wesley-1872-edition/sermon-43-the-scripture-way-of-salvation/.

[11] Dallas Willard, *The Spirit of the Disciplines: Understanding How God Changes Lives* (New York: HarperCollins, 1988), 37.

[12] Scot McKnight, *A Fellowship of Differents: Showing the World God's Design for Life Together* (Grand Rapids, MI: Zondervan, 2014), Kindle edition, 137.

[13] Ibid., 143.

[14] Willard, *The Spirit of the Disciplines*, 28.

[15] John 5:21

[16] John 5:24

[17] John 6:51

[18] 1 John 5:12

[19] John Wesley, Sermon 74, "Of the Church," in *The Sermons of John Wesley*, ed. Thomas Jackson, The Wesley Center for Applied Theology, accessed March 9, 2017, http://wesley.nnu.edu/john-wesley/the-sermons-of-john-wesley-1872-edition/sermon-74-of-the-church/.

[20] As quoted by Todd Hunter, "Dallas Willard, Jesus freak," *Joel J. Miller*, published May 9, 2013, http://www.patheos.com/blogs/joeljmiller/2013/05/dallas-willard-jesus-freak-todd-hunter-remembers-his-friend-mentor/.

[21] E. Stanley Jones, *Growing Spiritually* "Festival ed." (Nashville: Abingdon Press, 1953), 53.

[22] Ruth Haley Barton, *Sacred Rhythms: Arranging Our Lives for Spiritual Transformation* (Downers Grove, Ill: InterVarsity Press, 2006), 12.

[23] Eugene H. Peterson, "The Jesus Way: What is it? Why do I care?" (presentation at *The Jesus Way: Recovering the Lost Content of Discipleship* Renovaré International Conference on Spiritual Renewal, San Antonio, TX, June 21-24, 2009).

[24] "A Covenant Prayer in the Wesleyan Tradition" *The United Methodist Hymnal : Book of United Methodist Worship* (Nashville: The United Methodist Publishing House, 1989), 607.

[25] Teilhard de Chardin, "Prayer of Teilhard de Chardin: Patient Trust" *IgnatianSpirituality.com,* accessed October 21, 2015, http://www.ignatianspirituality.com/8078/prayer-of-theilhard-de-chardin.

[26] 1 Corinthians 15:10.

[27] John Wesley, Sermon 85, "On Working Out Our Own Salvation," in *The Sermons of John Wesley*, ed. Thomas Jackson, The Wesley Center for Applied Theology, accessed March 9, 2017, http://wesley.nnu.edu/john-wesley/the-sermons-of-john-wesley-1872-edition/sermon-85-on-working-out-our-own-salvation/.

[28] Willard, *The Great Omission*, 166.

[29] John Wesley, Sermon 16, "The Means of Grace," in *The Sermons of John Wesley*, ed. Thomas Jackson, The Wesley Center for Applied Theology, accessed October 23, 2014, http://wesley.nnu.edu/john-wesley/the-sermons-of-john-wesley-1872-edition/sermon-16-the-means-of-grace/.

[30] Dallas Willard, *The Divine Conspiracy: Rediscovering Our Hidden Life in God* (New York: HarperCollins, 1998), 234.

[31] Sören Kierkegaard, *Purity of Heart Is to Will One Thing*, Public Domain.

32 Psalm 23:1.

33 2 Corinthians 12:9.

34 James Bryan Smith, *The Good and Beautiful Life: Putting on the Character of Christ* (Downers Grove, IL: InterVarsity Press, 2009), 205-206.

35 Luke 11:1-4, as translated in N.T. Wright, *The Kingdom New Testament: A Contemporary Translation* (New York: HarperCollins, 2011).

36 *The Didache: The Teaching of the Twelve Apostles* (Orkos Press, 2014), 15.

37 See Numbers chapters 13 and 14.

38 Two invaluable guides for me have been Ruth Haley Barton, *Invitation to Solitude and Silence: Experiencing God's Transforming Presence* (Downer's Grove, IL: InterVarsity Press, 2004) and Martin Laird, *Into the Silent Land: A Guide to the Christian Practice of Contemplation* (New York: Oxford University Press, 2006).

39 Saint Augustine, "Sermon 8, On the Third Commandment," in *The Works of St. Augustine III*, 1, trans. E. Hill (Brooklyn, NY: New City Press), 244, as quoted in Laird, *Into the Silent Land*, 51-52.

40 Laird's *Into the Silent Land* contains a masterful description of how our distractions become our allies in developing our awareness of God.

41 See Acts 17:28.

42 John 15:4.

43 Willard has variations of this statement in multiple places. One is, "Prayer: Interactive conversation with God about what we and God are thinking and doing together." *The Life with God Bible* (New York: HarperCollins, 2005), 520.

[44] This kind of prayer of review is a simple form of the classic practices of the examination of consciousness and the examination of conscience. Many good resources are available as guides for regularly practicing this kind of prayer, notably:
- Ruth Haley Barton, "Self-Examination: Bringing My Whole Self Before God: *Sacred Rhythms*, 91-109.
- Audio-guided prayers of examen from *Pray As You Go*, http://pray-as-you-go.org/index.php?id=131.

[45] Wesley, "Means of Grace".

[46] Dallas Willard, *The Allure of Gentleness: Defending the Faith in the Manner of Jesus* (New York: HarperCollins, 2015), Kindle Edition, 105.

[47] Psalm 119:103.

[48] Psalm 119:131.

[49] Psalm 19:10.

[50] Psalm 1:1a, 2.

[51] Willard states, "You may have been told that it is good to read the Bible through every year and that you can ensure this will happen by reading so many verses per day from the Old and New Testaments. If you do this you may enjoy the reputation of one who reads the Bible through each year, and you may congratulate yourself on it. But will you become more like Christ and more filled with the life of God?... It is better in one year to have ten good verses transferred into the substance of our lives than to have every word of the Bible flash before our eyes." *Hearing God: Developing a Conversational Relationship with God* (Downers Grove, IL: InterVarsity Press, 1999), 163.

[52] Eugene H. Peterson, *Eat This Book: A Conversation in the Art of Spiritual Reading* (Grand Rapids, MI: Wm. B. Eerdmans, 2006), 82.

[53] John 5:37-40.

[54] M. Robert Mulholland, Jr., *Shaped by the Word: The Power of Scripture in Spiritual Formation* (Nashville: The Upper Room, 1985), 54.

[55] For further guidance on *lectio divina,* see Ruth Haley Barton, Chapter Three: "Scripture: Encountering God Through Lectio Divina," in *Sacred Rhythms.* Also Peterson, *Eat This Book.*

[56] Luke 14:12. Hat tip to Dallas Willard on this one. See *The Divine Conspiracy*, 108-109.

[57] 1 Timothy 5:23.

[58] Luke 16:9.

[59] Matthew 23:15.

[60] Romans 14:2.

[61] Peterson, *Eat This Book*, 58.

[62] Scot McKnight, *The Blue Parakeet: Rethinking How You Read the Bible* (Grand Rapids, MI: Zondervan, 2008), 54-74.

[63] Ibid., 59.

[64] Ibid., 60.

[65] https://www.christianbook.com/2018-bible-verses-mini-day-calendar/9781449484859/pd/484859, accessed April 8, 2017.

[66] McKnight, *The Blue Parakeet*, 62.

[67] Ibid., 65.

[68] Ibid., 65.

[69] Ibid., 71.

[70] Peterson, *Eat This Book*, 66.

[71] McKnight, *The Blue Parakeet*, 73.

72 Ibid., 74.

73 Peterson, *Eat This Book,* 48.

74 McKnight, *The Blue Parakeet,* 82.

75 N.T. Wright, *Scripture and the Authority of God: How to Read the Bible Today* (New York: HarperCollins, 2005), 121-127.

76 When I use the term "lectionary" in this chapter, I am referring to the Revised Common Lectionary, although other lectionaries are also available and useful. Information on the Revised Common Lectionary can be found at www.commontexts.org.

77 Rueben P. Job, *A Guide to Prayer for Ministers and Other Servants* (Nashville: The Upper Room, 1983).

78 A great place to start for readable commentaries is the *For Everyone* series, published by Westminster John Knox Press. The volumes on the Old Testament are written by John Goldingay, and the New Testament by N.T. Wright.

79 Rueben P. Job, *A Guide to Prayer for All Who Walk with God* (Nashville: Upper Room Books, 2013).

80 Wesley, "Means of Grace."

81 Willard, *The Great Omission,* 130.

82 John 15:4-8.

[83] I do not mean to imply with this statement that all experiences of "dryness" are due to a lack of cooperation on our part. Although that is the cause sometimes, at other times we may be genuinely open and cooperative when the experience of dryness comes. This can often be a good and healthy (though often not enjoyable) part of the process of learning to love God more purely, and is attested to throughout the Christian spiritual tradition. See, for example, Thomas H. Green, S.J., *When the Well Runs Dry: Prayer Beyond the Beginnings* (Notre Dame, IN: Ave Maria Press, 1979).

[84] Tom Wright, *The Meal Jesus Gave Us* (Louisville: Westminster John Knox, 2002), 6.

[85] *The United Methodist Hymnal*, 14.

[86] Steve Harper, *Devotional Life in the Wesleyan Tradition* (Nashville: The Upper Room, 1983), 37.

[87] *The United Methodist Hymnal*, 14.

[88] "Wesleyan Core Term: Lord's Supper," *Wesley Study Bible* (Nashville: Abingdon Press, 2009), 1401.

[89] N.T. Wright expresses this idea often, of the future coming to meet us in the present through Christ. *The Meal Jesus Gave Us* is one writing which expresses this important idea.

[90] *The United Methodist Hymnal*, 14.

[91] Willard, *The Divine Conspiracy*, 378.

[92] Wright, *The Meal Jesus Gave Us*, 56-57.

[93] Matthew 26:29.

[94] 1 John 3:2b, emphasis added.

[95] Revelation 19:9.

[96] J. Brent Bill, *Holy Silence: The Gift of Quaker Spirituality* (Brewster, MA: Paraclete Press, 2005), 3.

97 Henri J. M. Nouwen, "Moving From Solitude to Community," *Leadership Journal,* accessed January 5, 2016, http://www.christianitytoday.com/pastors/1995/spring/51280.html.

98 Henri J. M. Nouwen, *The Genesee Diary: Report from a Trappist Monastery* (New York: Image, 1989), 46. As quoted in Wil Hernandez, *Mere Spirituality: The Spiritual Life According to Henri Nouwen* (Woodstock, VT: Skylight Paths Publishing, 2015), 7.

99 For brief guidelines on what to do during a day of solitude with God, see my blog post, "How to Spend a Day Alone with God" at http://www.salvationlife.com/blog/how-to-spend-a-day-alone-with-god.

100

101 Wesley, "The Scripture Way of Salvation".

102 Willard, *The Spirit of the Disciplines*, ix.

103 For the term "you-ier," I am indebted to John Ortberg, *The Me I Want to Be.* For example: "Here is the good news: When you flourish, you become more you. You become more that person God had in mind when he thought you up. You don't just become holier. You become you-ier. You will change; God wants you to become a 'new creation.' But 'new' doesn't mean completely different; instead, it's like an old piece of furniture that gets restored to its intended beauty."

Ortberg, *The Me I Want to Be: Becoming God's Best Version of You* (Grand Rapids, MI: Zondervan, 2009), 16.

[104] The theological term in many Christian traditions, particularly my own Wesleyan/Methodist tradition, for the fullness/maturity/holiness that I am trying to describe in this chapter (and indeed through the whole book) is "Christian Perfection," although I never name it in the chapter. While it is expressly what I am trying to describe, I am intentionally trying to use other language to describe the same reality to let the chapter be as acceptable as possible across the Christian ecumenical spectrum.

[105] Matthew 5:48.

[106] Gordon T. Smith, *Called to be Saints: An Invitation to Christian Maturity* (Downers Grove, IL: InterVarsity Press, 2014).

[107] Ibid., 64.

[108] Ibid., 89.

[109] Ibid., 91.

[110] See John chapters 14-17.

[111] See Willard, *The Divine Conspiracy*, 62-64.

[112] Ibid., 244-245.

[113] Ibid., 62.

[114] James Bryan Smith, *Room of Marvels* (Nashville: B&H Publishing Group, 2007), Kindle Edition, Location 418.

[115] The images of the good shirt and guitar come from one of my favorite songs: "Stuff That Works" by Guy Clark. When heard through the lens of our lives with God, it helps us recharacterize this idea of holiness as having to do with serving the intended purpose of our Creator. See Guy Clark, "Stuff That Works" in *Dublin Blues*, Asylum, 1995.

116 The following athletic metaphor is adapted from similar uses by Willard, *The Spirit of the Disciplines*, 3-4, and Gary Moon, "Tennis Anyone," *Conversations Journal*, accessed February 18, 2012, http://conversationsjournal.com/2011/04/tennis-anyone/.

117 Colossians 3:3-4.

118 Wesley, "Preface" to *Hymns and Sacred Poems*, accessed March 10, 2017 at *Eighteenth Century Collections Online*, http://quod.lib.umich.edu/e/ecco/004800840.0001.000/1:2?rgn=div1;view=fulltext.

119 Ibid.

120 Albert Haase, O.F.M., *Coming Home to Your True Self: Leaving the Emptiness of False Attractions* (Downers Grove, IL: InterVarsity Press, 2008), 130-135.

121 This is a translation attributed to the *Talmud*, though it apparently may not be the best translation. See "Mazal Tov!: Some Thoughts on Growing Pains," *Coffee Shop Rabbi*, accessed March 12, 2017, https://coffeeshoprabbi.com/2015/03/24/mazal-tov-some-thoughts-on-growing-pains/

122 John Wesley, Sermon 74, "Of the Church" in *The Sermons of John Wesley*, ed. Thomas Jackson, The Wesley Center for Applied Theology, accessed March 12, 2017, http://wesley.nnu.edu/john-wesley/the-sermons-of-john-wesley-1872-edition/sermon-74-of-the-church/.

123 Dallas Willard, *Living in Christ's Presence: Final Words on Heaven and the Kingdom of God* (Downers Grove, IL: InterVarsity Press, 2014), 21.

124 See John 21:15-19.

125 For the concept of "the wall," and the ideas that led me to develop these three stages of experience in the church, I am indebted to the excellent work, Janet O. Hagberg and Robert A. Guelich, *The Critical Journey: Stages in the Life of Faith* (Salem, Wis: Sheffield Publishing, 1995).

126 This community experience was the Transforming Community (see http://www.transformingcenter.org), and the teacher was Ruth Haley Barton.

127 Willard said, "Pastors need to redefine success. The popular model of success involves the ABCs—attendance, buildings, and cash. Instead of counting Christians, we need to weigh them. We weigh them by focusing on the most important kind of growth—love, joy, peace, longsuffering, gentleness, goodness, kindness, and so on—fruit in keeping with the gospel and the kingdom."

"The Apprentices," *dwillard.org*, accessed March 12, 2017, http://www.dwillard.org/articles/artview.asp?artID=112.

128 Willard says, "We may not soon have bigger crowds around us—and in fact they may for a while even get smaller—but we will soon have bigger Christians for sure. This is what I call 'church growth for those who hate it.' And bigger crowds are sure to follow, for the simple reason that human beings desperately need what we bring to them, the word and reality of The Kingdom Among Us."

The Divine Conspiracy, 373.

129 Stephen Neill, *Christian Holiness* (New York: Harper and Row, 1960), 114-15. As quoted in Gordon T. Smith, *Called to be Saints*, 184.

130 John Wesley, Sermon 52, "The Reformation of Manners" in *The Sermons of John Wesley*, ed. Thomas Jackson, The Wesley Center for Applied Theology, accessed March 12, 2017, http://wesley.nnu.edu/john-wesley/the-sermons-of-john-wesley-1872-edition/sermon-52-the-reformation-of-manners/.

131 Dallas Willard, *The Spirit of the Disciplines*, 241.

132 M. Robert Mulholland, Jr., *The Deeper Journey: The Spirituality of Discovering Your True Self* (Downers Grove, IL: InterVarsity Press, 2006), 47-48.

133 M. Robert Mulholland, Jr., *Invitation to a Journey: A Road Map for Spiritual Formation* (Downers Grove, IL: InterVarsity Press, 1993), 23.

134 See Mulholland, *The Deeper Journey*, 47-48.

135 Matthew 7:21-23.

136 See Resurrection Health of Memphis, Tennessee at http://www.rezhealth.org.

137 See International Justice Mission at http://www.ijm.org. This description of their practice of silence is found in Ruth Haley Barton, *Strengthening the Soul of Your Leadership: Seeking God in the Crucible of Ministry* (Downers Grove, IL: InterVarsity Press, 2008), 130-132.

138 Willard, *The Spirit of the Disciplines*, 241.

139 Matthew 7:21-23.

140 I am indebted to a thought expressed in a personal note from Fr. Albert Hasse, who said, "I like to think of grace as 'God's voracious enthusiasm' to be in a relationship with us. What attracts me so much about that description is that it gets away from the idea...that grace is a 'thing' like a divine liquid that God pours into our souls."

51784692R00113

Made in the USA
San Bernardino, CA
01 August 2017